WHEN THE LORD SPOKE
and other adventures of a California boyhood

PHIL BOWHAY

ISBN: 1-4392-0333-4
ISBN-13: 9781439203330

Visit www.booksurge.com to order additional copies.

Landscape Press
833 Topper Lane
Lafayette, CA 94549

Some items previously printed in Monterey Herald
and reprinted here with permission.
Cover Art by James Herrera/Monterey Herald

Printed in U.S.A.

First printing: August 2008

Library of Congress data TK

WHEN THE LORD SPOKE
and other adventures of a California boyhood

CONTENTS

For Susie

Acknowledgments

I am especially grateful to my mom, who told me seventy-five years ago that everybody wanted to hear everything I said, and to my dad, who not only tolerated but also encouraged me. My writing, however, didn't see the light of day until Royal Calkins at the *Monterey Herald* printed my first real story, "When the Lord Spoke," about parked-car petting under the foghorn, and has printed dozens since. Joanie Zischke, sadly no longer with us, was my best early critic. She liked everything I wrote!

There's nothing like a fan base to keep you at the computer, and I give heartfelt thanks to Barbara Podoloff @ Copies By-The-Sea, Helen and Beau Breck, Mary and John Ricksen, Hans Lehman, Mae McCoy, Karen Juhring, Trudy Post, Dan Albert, Mary Fry, Colette O'Connor, Don and Jayne Gasperson, Jim and Rita deLorimier, Honey and Ray Pere, Marie Rosenblatt, sweet Annie Richerts, and everybody else who ever went to Pacific Grove High School. Jim Vorhes deserves credit and a free drink for a great letter to the *Herald*. Thanks, too, to Terri Hinte, who smoothed out the syntax and sanded with a fine eye and hand where necessary.

Special thanks to my sweetheart, Susie Pearson, who reads all my stuff and lays on lavish praise, pulling me through periods of "block." My kids Scott and Carrie, my sister Shirley, and my brothers Mike and Tom are adoring fans, but big-time, special gratitude goes to my daughter, Laura Shumaker, who has put all this stuff together, taking up with encouragement where my mom left off! Her hard work on her own book, *A Regular Guy*, was a real inspiration.

Finally, I write more for fame than fortune, but a little fortune wouldn't hurt. If you bought this book, I thank you. If you didn't, remember: Christmas is coming, and it would make a fine gift!

—*Phil Bowhay*

Introduction

Well!, you might ask. What is *this* all about?

It's a little bit of a lot of things. Some of these stories are columns printed in the *Monterey Herald*. Others are throwaway essays, some fiction based on observation, some commentary.

Just in case you don't know, the Monterey Peninsula is on the coast of Central California, about a hundred miles south of San Francisco on Monterey Bay. Rich in history and natural beauty, the three towns of Monterey, Carmel, and Pacific Grove each have their own special charms and quirks. We love tourists—guests— and they love us. Sure, just call ahead and I'd *love* to show you around. Might even buy lunch!

Pacific Grove, or PG, is called "The Last Hometown," which seems a little pretentious, but close enough. The current "big deals" on the Peninsula are Pebble Beach, the Aquarium, Cannery Row, Laguna Seca races, 17 Mile Drive, and Carmel's former mayor, Clint Eastwood. In the old days we had Fort Ord, the Presidio, Del Monte Hotel, and lots of bohemians, whatever they were.

And now, of course, there's me!

I. GROWING UP

Chapter 1
When the Lord Spoke

Back in the old days, the 1940s, I don't remember ever hearing the term "petting" (though we *were* in Pacific Grove, a little buffered from the rest of the world). There was, however, the widely accepted and practiced art of "necking." Now and then our parents giggled about "spooning" or "sparking" in *their* old days, but I thought that was something different.

As lusty teenagers, neck we did with only occasional embarrassment or consequence. Nowadays we read with fascination and wonder about varying practices of "safe sex," which seems to be either a redundancy or a contradiction. We also note more discussion of accidental or unwanted consequences, such as pregnancy or other emotional distress, than we endured long ago.

Our simple and highly anticipated routine usually started with a dance in the high school gym or the Scout Hall, then off to Lover's Point café for a quick bite to eat. All this assumes we had use of the family car. Since it was probably a moonlit or starlit night, we might drive out to the Point to watch the waves. (What could be more romantic than the sound of the surf, the pungent odor of rotting kelp, the soft waft of Arrid and White Shoulders?) And then, we would commence to *neck*. Part of the thrill—and possible restraint—was the not uncommon visit of a voyeuristic cop with a very bright flashlight. "Just looking," he'd tell us.

Passion is fragile, of course, even in those teenage years. While the mood was enhanced by soft sounds from the radio, such as "Moonlight Becomes You" or "Stardust," it was invariably broken when the station would sign off with either "The Star Spangled Banner" or, worse yet, by God, "The Lord's Prayer"! That would send us home, a tender kiss at the front door amid the sweet agony of "Goodnight, Sweetheart."

But the sobering effect of the National Anthem or "The Lord's Prayer" was temporary. A few nights later, we were right back at the Point, watching the surf and holding hands, so to speak.

One night, we had parked on the left side of the road instead of the surf side. The view was spectacular, the moon and stars at their very best, filling us with hope and promise. As we innocently snuggled and breathed sweet sounds, the gear shift a minor inconvenience, we did not see the fog come in. Wet and dripping, the fog rose from the bay and shrouded the moon and the windshield. Passion was hardly dampened, but rather heightened to a point near fulfillment.

Then came a sound like no other. It was crushing, overwhelming, defeating. A roar from hell, it rattled our bones, shook our teeth, tightened our braces, and loosened our fillings. We had unwittingly parked right under and next to the most powerful foghorn in the known world. It was doing its duty, warning those in peril at sea (not to mention those parked at the Point). For us it was the voice of God, judgmental and signaling damnation, not only cooling passions and shrinking desire, but informing the world that innocent sins were not permitted on this stretch of Pacific Coast.

There was a two-second blast, a five-second interval, another blast, a twenty-four-second interval, and the Lord spoke again, ever louder, it seemed, than before. By the third chorus, some girls were known to cry, while boys, still shaken, cursed their bad luck.

Up and down the Point engines revved, lights came on. As the foghorn continued to blast away, we meekly drove home.

That old foghorn has been quiet for years now, but it should be preserved, as a monument to those ships saved by its warning roars, not to mention those of us saved from the costs of early pseudo-sin and what might have happened had the fog not rolled in.

Chapter 2
An Abominable Shrub

If you haven't had poison oak, you haven't lived. At least you haven't lived on the Monterey Peninsula.

I suspect more has been written about PO than HIV. Robert Louis Stevenson probably said it most succinctly in *The Silverado Squatters*: "In all woods and by every wayside there prospers an abominable shrub or weed, called poison oak, whose very neighborhood is venomous to some, and whose actual touch is avoided by the most impervious."

Now if you want to share some misery and bond with those who have suffered before, just take a walk in the woods. I bring this up since my dog recently romped around Flanders Mansion. Having petted, praised, and hugged her—"Good dog! You came back!"—I got that tell-tale itch with the tiny blisters and oozing misery the next morning. It had been several years since I'd had that particular suffering, but there was no doubt about the diagnosis.

We are blessed in these modern times with cortisone-laced creams and potions that ease the itch and shorten the insult, but friends, it still isn't worth the experience. I should add that if you have to pee after even *possible* exposure, do not touch. . . well, you get the picture. I remember as a Boy Scout, I—but that's another story.

Mr. Tuttle, Pacific Grove's pioneer pharmacist, knew a gold mine when he saw it: he whipped up a Poison Oak Lotion. It did absolutely no good, except for the alcohol which covered the itch with a welcome sting, but that didn't last. Calamine lotion, dabbed on with cotton, seemed to do even less than Tuttle's. The most insane home remedy was gasoline, of all things, rubbed on the blisters and ooze. The burn was even worse than the itch and a bit dangerous, too. As I recall, the folk favorite was Clorox straight from the jug. A girl I met one summer later told me that the thing she remembered most about me was that I smelled like either a swimming pool or her mother's washing machine. Very clean, but not very romantic.

Given time, the blisters and itch did fade away, and we would swear again to spend time on the beach instead of in the woods. But let's be fair to poison oak. Spectacular in the fall when that glossy green turns a brilliant red, it's beautiful to see but dangerous to touch. Just like some women we've all known—but that, too, is another story.

Chapter 3
Christmas Tree

Back in the late 1930s, my dad, Lowell Bowhay, was the forest ranger in Kernville, in the southern end of the Sierra on the Kern River above Bakersfield. Mid-November was Christmas tree–cutting time, and Dad always had requests from headquarters for a good selection of silver-tips. He took his crew, with me tagging along, up the road on Greenhorn Mountain. Since he patrolled the mountain all year, he knew where the best trees were. Sometimes, working through early snow, they cut dozens and trucked them off to Bakersfield for distribution to friends of the county.

In 1939 he got a call earlier than usual and was asked to find the tallest, most perfect tree on the mountain. I remember riding and hiking with him as he found and noted several fine specimens, but none were perfect. Some were too thin, others too short or bent by years of snow and wind. We went farther up the mountain, and finally, after several days, about a half mile off the road he found the one he wanted. It was very tall, straight, and graceful with full branches perfectly placed from the base to the spire at the top.

The tree was carefully cut and felled so as to protect the branches. A full crew dragged it to the road and with winches loaded it on a huge semitrailer truck. Down the mountain went the tree, to the river road and then to Bakersfield. Then, to protect its length and shape, it was loaded on *two* railroad flat cars.

Its journey continued up the Valley, and across to Oakland, then onto a huge barge, across the Bay. And then, and *then*: its final destination, Treasure Island and the 1939 World's Fair! Up it went, with fanfare and celebration. Finally, with a thousand lights, it could be seen and admired across the Bay, and who knows, maybe around the world!

Chapter 4
Survival, Sort Of

I must confess that I come from a long line of law-infringers.

No, I should rephrase that and explain. I refer to some long-ago Fish and Game laws, things like extending the season by a day or two, or those lucky days taking a couple of trout over the limit, or fudging a quarter-inch on a Pismo clam. These minor sins, committed by my dad and my uncles, were balanced by days when not a single fish was caught, nor a single clam raked out of the sand, not to mention those hunting seasons never used.

Keep in mind that the Bowhays were pioneers and homesteaders in the Gold Country and San Joaquin Valley, never catching or killing for anything other than food. You may also remember shortages during World War II, when meat, among other things, was rationed. Well, that's all history now, and no excuses! Just look at what you can get at Costco, and no limit on those Rainbow beauties, farmed or otherwise. And of course, you can still shoot a deer in season, if you really must have that fresh liver.

It was that craving for liver those many years ago that took my dad to the woods—in season, as I recall—up behind what is now Del Monte Center. An excellent shot, he waited quietly in the poison oak. And then, through the brush, in a panic, came a doe with her fawn at her side, running for their lives. Just a few yards behind, and gaining, came a big Doberman with obvious evil intent. Dad, of course, shot the Doberman. Bambi and the doe ran on to higher ground without looking back.

No. I know what you're thinking. We had macaroni and cheese for dinner.

Uncle Les was another good shot, but he didn't waste a bullet unless he had to. Up on the shores of Huntington Lake, in the Sierra behind Fresno, the residents kept stands near the cabins and set out cabbages for the deer. One autumn afternoon an old doe, who Uncle Les claimed was well along in years and vulnerable to mountain lion attack, moved up the path to taste the cabbage. Les claimed it was really a mercy killing, and he dispatched her with a baseball bat to the head. (He had batted .380 his last season at Hanford High.) He hauled the carcass into the cabin and was happily butchering when out the window he saw the game warden slowly walking up the trail from the road. Well, it was hindquarter in the oven, forequarter under the bed, odds and ends in a washtub, then under the sink. He mopped up any blood with a gunnysack and tossed it out the back window.

"Well hi, warden! Come on in for a cup of coffee!"

Sad to tell, but Uncle Les had left the head on the sink. He was banned from the forest for a few years, but later, by golly, worked for the Fish and Game, planting trout in the High Country.

Since I am neither a pioneer nor a homesteader I am a strong, even fervent believer in game laws and bag limits. *Shoot a quail, go to jail!* And let's face it, just about the only things there's more of left—aside from people—are deer and raccoons.

Did my dad and uncles bend a law now and then? Hey, wait a minute! Didn't I see you going seventy in a fifty-five zone?

Chapter 5
In the Sweet Bye and Bye

Those lovely old ladies of Pacific Grove, the ones that still remembered New England, are gone now. Gone with the sand dunes, the Del Monte Express, the foghorn, and the old Methodist Church. If you grew up in PG in the 1930s and '40s, you remember them. They had a certain charm and class that you don't see much anymore.

They came to our "Piney Paradise" with family or friends to worship Jesus, something like the Puritans that many claimed as ancestors. They were quietly religious without being pious and could still recite verses and pithy sayings. ("The faults of our neighbors with freedom we blame, but we tax not ourselves though we practice the same," and on and on.)

You can see their names on those elderly cottages and the more spacious houses as well, those present-day bed and breakfasts and compact restaurants. Their generations were a bridge of sorts between those Victorians in the Hathaway photos and the postwar era, a time when we seemed to briefly turn our attention away from our local history.

They had strong opinions and healthy bodies, descended from pioneer stock and New England whaling families. With a few exceptions, I suspect, they were kind and generous, supporting their churches and needy neighbors. They swept their sidewalks, not stopping at the curb, and washed their milk bottles.

Their names were almost lyrical, from a romantic tradition: Eglantine, Flora Belle, Sue Estelle, and from a slightly later vintage, Elmarie.

Certain traditions or social habits were common. Most of them knitted, tatted, embroidered, or otherwise sewed. Despite the fact that card games were frowned upon, even illegal, other table games were popular. Care for a little Parcheesi, backgammon, or dominoes?

For some reason other than habit, most of the ladies had dishes of horehound candy. A brown, sugar-dusted drop with alleged curative powers, it tasted awful. Sort of a cross between burnt coffee, cod liver oil, and used cat litter. Don't try it.

Despite the horehound, most of these lovely old-lady houses were not only interesting, but in some cases downright fascinating. After all, they were entitled to certain oddities or idiosyncrasies, and aren't we all.

Mrs. Swann lived up 18th above Laurel, brown shingles, a ratty palm tree in the front yard, and a jungle of split-leaf philodendron in the entry hall. The place was always stuffy hot, gas heater hissing in the corner, horehound in the cut-glass dish on the doily-covered table, and a cat, of course, sleeping on a love seat near the window.

I would have forgotten all this except for the icon on her fireplace mantle: a clear glass bottle, about six inches tall, filled with formaldehyde and her dead mother's ring finger, complete with wedding ring. The finger was tied with a small bow at the base and had a pale fingernail at the top. No flowers to soften the image, no picture of the departed, just an otherwise bare mantle with Mama's digit. While Mrs. Swann explained casually what this was and then moved on to other things, I was transfixed and stared at this thing without comment. My mother, who was just as fascinated, and possibly repelled, had the sense not to tell me not to stare. And horehound or not, I always looked forward to visits at Mrs. Swann's. I don't remember if there were any offspring of Mrs. Swann's who might have inherited the finger, but would rather hope that it was buried along with Mrs. Swann, unless, of course, she was herself preserved in some other unorthodox manner.

Miss Preble, whose grandfather, Commodore Preble, battled the Barbary pirates from the USS Constitution, Old Ironsides, was filled with grand stories of peril at sea, maple syrup, and Indians, both friendly and fierce. The Tuck sisters read tea leaves and forecast the future from the depths of a crystal ball. They painted seascapes and tended houseplants in the late stages of life. They played piano duets and sang hymns happily off-key.

They still had iceboxes, coolers, and Franklin stoves. They walked to the store and church and back. Tuttle delivered drugs when necessary, Borchers dropped off hunks of coal, and Dr. Hoyt made house calls if they ever got sick. Dr. Hoyt was something of a celebrity to the ladies, having removed his own appendix when he was a missionary in Korea. "Here, Dr. Hoyt! Have some more horehound drops!"

The DAR—Daughters of the American Revolution, if you didn't know—possibly had more members in Pacific Grove than in Boston. The ladies brought out bunting and American flags on every holiday. They sang "The Battle Hymn" and "Tramp, Tramp, Tramp" with fervor. Some were widows, some maiden ladies, all with memories of a long time ago.

There seemed to be a lot of them. My dad, somewhat irreverently, called PG the Old Lady Capital of the World. He said they came here to die, but never did. Well yes, they did, Dad. They're all gone now.

Chapter 6
Uncle Les

Uncle Les, Leslie Newton Bowhay, was my favorite uncle. I had only one other, Harold, and I don't count Uncle Linn, Aunt Verna's husband. Les was big, with a booming voice and a big belly. Mom explained that this was because he was gassed during the war—World War I. Les was big and kind, always pleasant to us kids.

He didn't have any children of his own, although story is he had to leave his home in Hanford for a couple of years having been too friendly with one of the local ladies. Les always claimed it was a case of mistaken identity, but nevertheless, off to Coalinga where he worked as a roughneck. Coalinga must have been pretty wild in those days, and I think Les did just fine.

Les was never out of line, so to speak, but one of his trademarks was his ability to swear, almost lyrically. My mother claimed that Les could swear funny, but Harold always swore dirty. Les's best line, said Mom, came after he had viewed a particularly poor paint job on one of the county's projects: "I could have done better with a mop and a bucket of shit!" This oft- repeated remark was always greeted with hilarity by the ladies, a real pants-wetter, if you will.

Uncle Harold seemed to be cut from a slightly different cloth. He was recognized as the smartest of the sibs, not counting Morris (who was brilliant, by all accounts, but died young, and I never knew him). Harold married Aunt Evelyn when he was in his early fifties, but he'd had several attachments in the years preceding.

I remember my fifth-grade teacher in Bakersfield, Miss Long. She seemed old to me at the time, but that was just my inexperienced perspective. I think Harold had dropped her during the summer, which may have explained her general crabbiness.

Each of us had blue spelling books, with a California poppy on the cover. We also had desks with inkwells and lids that lifted up in front of us. On a regular basis Miss Long would go into a rage of sorts, possibly brought on by some kid. She would take her copy of the speller and throw it across the classroom, aiming at the miscreant. Whenever she raised her speller, every kid knew what was happening and, in unison, all of our desktops flew up! This seemed to calm her down, and she would then say in even tones, "You may all put your heads down on your desks."

Harold had, indeed, made a wise decision.

Chapter 7
Beans for Breakfast,
or Hominy Hearts Have You Broken

Food means love, of course, but in the Bowhay house it also meant fun and family, with everybody pitching in, one way or another, in the kitchen. We all learned to cook early, sometimes from each other, but usually from Mom and Dad.

Mom grew up with the Philbricks and their New England recipes, enhanced and honed by the Pacific Grove church kitchens. Dad was a firehouse chef, with a pioneer culinary background, also influenced by old rural Southern cooking that Grandma Bowhay learned in the ranch kitchens of San Joaquin Valley. And then, of course, there were the basic California menus, with strong Mexican overtones, and the rich supply of seafood and Salinas Valley produce.

Dad was also a hunter, and since we always ate what he caught or killed, he didn't pay a lot of attention to bag limits or seasons. This was also true of his brothers, and none of them had any patience with poachers who had no regard for what they killed.

Once upon a time we had had a marginally successfully quail shoot behind the airport. Driving back by the antenna arrays, we spotted a flock of birds on the grass.

"Stop, boys," said Dad. "I think those are Golden Plover! Against the law, but they're supposed to be good eating!"

Well, we popped one, scooped it up, and carried it home. Don't know to this day if it was a Golden Plover, but it certainly wasn't good to eat. We gave it a decent burial in the backyard.

Uncle Les worked for the Fish and Game one summer, a long time ago, carrying tanks of trout fingerlings on mule back into the Sierra for planting in high-altitude lakes.

He said that most nights they would scoop a cup or two, fry them up, and eat "guts, feathers, and all." Delicious!

Back in the '30s and '40s, and even a little in the '50s, Pismos, the finest of all clams, were plentiful on the Coast, and not just on the beach south of here that's named for them. In Monterey Bay the beds seemed to start just north of the Salinas River and run up on the beaches almost to Santa Cruz. Early on the limits were so generous there was no need to break the law. Later, however, as those goddamn otters ate their fill, it became tougher to get enough for dinner.

I might mention that the small ones were especially tasty. Standing knee-deep with surf behind, I'd crack a three-inch Pismo on the handle of the clamming fork, then a quick rinse and down the hatch! The legal Pismos, as big as your hand, fried, are about as good as it gets. I can't forget the time my dad and I and Susie were clamming off Moss Landing, and we might have had a clam or two slightly undersized. Just to ensure no lurch with the law, Susie tucked three or four into her bra. She said they were cold.

Around the Bowhays', as everywhere else in town, cracked Dungeness was a real treat, no matter how often we had it, which was often. After dinner there was always a rush to the kitchen to retrieve the shells picked by the out-of-town guests, who never really understood the nooks and crannies. My sister Shirley was always the best scavenger, getting at least a pound of good crabmeat from the leavings. Okay, maybe half a pound.

Abalone was the best, even better than Pismos. One night Dad got up a little after midnight, went downstairs, and decided to make tamale pie. Easy enough, and why not? When you want tamale pie, nothing else will really do. As we smelled the sauce simmering, we all gradually got up and went downstairs, sat down with Mom and Dad, and ate.

Then Dad said, "Boys, I think we've got a good minus tide. Let's see if we can get some abalone." Off we went, cold and shivering, to Lover's Point, believe it or not. The tide was good and low, and right there in front of where Borg's is now, we each limited. They were all good size, and we must have cleaned and pounded for three hours when we got home. Boy, what a feed! And still a little tamale pie on the side.

Salmon fishing was always an adventure, and it made sense to me to buy it rather than go through the stress and strain of trolling endlessly across the bay. My dad, though, never missed a chance to go out. Once he went out on a friend's boat, along with Brooks, who told the story. About midmorning they hooked a ten-foot shark—exciting enough, but especially because there was a premium price running on shark liver, commercial license or not. After much sweating and swearing, they finally got the thing aboard. Sharks do not take kindly to such treatment, and it was raising hell; in fact, it was very dangerous. Dad, for unknown reasons, had a pistol in his pocket. He pulled it out, took dead aim, and shot the shark in the head. This further upset the shark, which then vomited on the deck. Of even more concern was the bullet hole in the bottom of the boat. Well, that was that. Over the side went the shark, liver and all, the seagulls thrilled with the mess. The hole was plugged, and the boat returned to the harbor. Dad bought a salmon, and all was well. Except for the shark, but what the hell.

But back to the kitchen. It seemed to me that Grandma Bowhay (Brooks) was always cooking, the kitchen steaming and rich with the smell of cooked stews of all kinds. These stews included chickens, of course, with a fascinating progression of tiny to mature eggs about to be laid. No matter, plenty of laying hens. And then the guinea fowl, turkeys (usually fried), and peacock! Grandma's cooking was primarily pioneer, with a touch of Southern on the edges. After all, she was born in a covered wagon in the middle of the Kings River, on Christmas Day many years ago. Her mother had come across the country on horseback, her father across the Isthmus. They met in the Gold Country and headed to the Valley when Grandma was born. The Brooks family settled around Hanford and for a long time lived on what they grew and could shoot.

Grandma's kitchen in Delano was the center of the house. It had two stoves—one gas, the other wood-burning, which she refused to give up.

I accepted the fact that string beans should be cooked for a long, long time, with pieces of bacon suffering in the same pot. So what if we did gag on the strings now and then.

One of Grandma's best was fried sowbelly, which was pretty close to uncured bacon. Hard to find now. The most talked-about dish was scrapple, cornmeal cooked with whatever was left over in the cooler. This always seemed to be liver, and hence the family name for it—crapple. Not good, even with syrup.

Best thing, though, were Grandma's sugar cookies: always there, always baking, always just right.

Dad brought along the tradition of what we now call "offal," and purely awful, even in those days. I never liked tripe, couldn't stand brains, and even had a hard time with sweetbreads but learned to love them later. Liver was a mixed blessing, usually cooked with bacon and onions, and really pretty good. Loved beef tongue, also hard to find today. We loved venison, especially in stews, and a real treat was venison liver, fresh from the day the deer was shot. The other cuts had to hang for a few days, but not the liver.

Speaking of beef tongue, here's one of my mom's favorite stories. A lady walked into a diner and asked the waiter what the special was. He told her Beef Tongue. "What!" she said. "Out of a dirty old cow's mouth! No thanks. Give me an egg sandwich."

High humor in Pacific Grove!

And then the produce. Fun to follow the lettuce trucks near Spreckels and pick up the heads that fell by the side of the road. And how much fun to watch our out-of-town guests tackle an artichoke! Give them a break after a chew or two.

I remember finding a dime at the bottom of the PG swimming pool, going to Holman's, and buying a cookbook. Later, with maybe a quarter, I bought the Duncan Hines cookbook, which I still have. I picked the simplest recipe in the book and made it for the family. A casserole of sweet potatoes and onions. Great supportive raves around the table, but it was absolutely vile! Never again, Mr. Hines!

When Mom cooked, she moved around the kitchen with a quiet, efficient grace. Never rushed, but never still. She seemed to be cooking three or four things at once, and indeed, our meals were never a one-dish affair. There was the main thing, of course, but always a side dish or two, and always a dessert. Meat was overcooked, at least by today's standards. My first taste of rare beef was at a Rotary Club barbecue, right after the war. Up to that point I thought all meat was tough! Salmon was usually boiled in cheesecloth, longer than necessary, and served with a rich egg sauce. Fried chicken, always fried with lard or Crisco, then

19

a tablespoon of water, covered for ten minutes, and to the table.

Desserts were cooked with ease. Pies just seemed routine. Cakes, of course. Mayonnaise cake, still one of the best (recipe to follow), and Gum Drop Fruit Cake (recipe to follow if I can find it). And then Persimmon Pudding, cooked in a coffee can, and served warm with "Hard Sauce."

In the summer, mustard pickles were a big item, and homemade sauerkraut! Sterilized Mason jars, shredded cabbage, salt, and hot water, sealed up for about a month, and nothing better.

During the war, meat was rationed, and hard to get in any case. Dad's good friend, Ernie Still, had a ranch down east of Paso Robles, and Dad arrived home one afternoon with a live sheep in the back seat of the car. Not a lamb. Just a sheep. It made considerable noise, but we got it down to the basement without interference from the neighbors or the law. Dad put it "out of its misery" with a quick blow to the head with the blunt end of my Boy Scout hatchet. He strung it up, skinned and butchered it out, and we ate mutton or lamb, depending on how it was cooked, for a week or two. We might have even invited a neighbor. We buried the guts in the backyard and had an especially fine crop of blackberries the following year.

Uncle Harold had a ranch east of Bakersfield on the Kern River. One of its huge high points for us was the wild mushroom crop after warm spring rains. These were the little white buttons—sometimes growing three or four inches across—with pink spores on the underside. This was an important distinction, since the look-alikes with the *white* spores were deadly. The best mushrooms grew right out of pies of cow manure, which may sound gross, but that's where Safeway mushrooms grow too. We'd head back to the ranch with buckets full, and then sautéed them in butter (fried, actually) with the whole mess turning black, and delicious.

Mushrooms are where you find them, and I've noticed millions growing in the hills between Cholame and Paso Robles. Looked like snow. I never stopped, but maybe next time.

We didn't eat a lot of pheasant, but when we did it was a real treat. Tastes like chicken. One evening we sat down to a dinner of two or three birds, fried and very good. In walked in a guy named Bates who had been fixing a broken window in one of the cottages. Bates, usually drunk, was a nice enough guy. Invited to sit down, he promptly started to clear the plate of pheasant. Hospitality is one thing; being taken advantage of is another. Dad said, "Excuse me, Bates," reached across, left Bates with a drumstick, and scooped the rest onto *his* plate, later to be shared with the family. Bates didn't bat an eye, finished the drumstick, and walked out the door. I don't think he remembered to send a bill for the window repair.

Mike likes to tell the lobster story. Somebody dropped off a gunnysack of lobsters one afternoon, cause for great excitement. Just about dinnertime, a bevy of babes—or a covey of girls, friends of Mike's or maybe Brooks's or Tom's (I was away at UNM)— stopped by to say hello, and by golly, they hadn't realized it was almost time to eat!

Mom and Dad, always perfect hosts, asked the gals to sit down and share the lobsters, since of *course* we had plenty. The guests ate with gusto, and sure enough, when all was said and done, Dad discovered there were none left for him. Better to give than to eat yourself; he just grinned, hoping the gals later expressed their gratitude to whomever they had come to visit.

Next morning Dad discovered two very dead lobsters in the bottom of the gunnysack, over the edge, so to speak.

Well, now. Here we are for the mayonnaise cake. There are several variations, but all of the same theme of a cup or so of Best Foods.

2 c. flour
½ c. cocoa
1½ tsp. baking soda
¼ tsp. salt
1 c. sugar
¾ c. mayonnaise
1 c. water
1 tsp. vanilla

Sift together the flour, cocoa, soda, and salt. Cream together the sugar, mayo, water, and vanilla. Add dry ingredients to the creamed mixture; stir until well blended. Pour batter into greased and floured layer-cake pans (or 9x13 pan). Bake at 350° for about 25 minutes. (You can also add raisins and/or nuts.) Any frosting will do.

Gum Drop Fruitcake? Any fruitcake recipe will do, but instead of the candied fruits, toss in pieces of gum drops—no spice drops or licorice, and there you have it!

Chapter 8
Kick the Can

I was eleven, maybe almost twelve, just before sex was invented, or at least, discovered, and I was in the kitchen with Mom. I told her I thought I was in love with Vivian, the girl down the street. She said that was nice, that it was probably "puppy love," and that Vivian was a very nice girl.

Vivian and I had been pals, "childhood friends," for as many years as eleven or twelve could handle, but somehow it was more delicious now to see her those summer months when she visited her grandparents.

That afternoon we played Kick the Can and we hid in the same place, in a place just behind the garage. We had hidden there before. Today, though, it was even more special. We had been running—you remember Kick the Can—and were a little sweaty. We stood close, and we looked at each other.

What puppy love has to do with Kick the Can is a stretch, but in quiet reverie one thing leads to another. Hide-and-Seek, of course, and Hit-the-Bat filled up summer afternoons. Then Mom called, "Supper's ready!" and that was it till tomorrow.

I could be wrong, but I don't think any of that happens anymore. The streets are crowded and busy, but you can still play catch on the sidewalks and shoot hoops. We didn't have video games in the old days. Didn't even have a TV! Matter of fact, my twenty-three-year-old honor student granddaughter didn't know what a phonograph was! (And the old gag, I told her to go to typewriter repair school, but she didn't listen. Became a nurse instead.)

Along about the eighth grade we tried Spin-the-Bottle once or twice. It seemed like a waste of time, with very uncertain results. We heard stories about things like Sardines, or Hide Together in a Closet, but thought those better left to kids from Carmel. We might have really missed something.

Digging around in a box of memories the other day, I found a bag of marbles. I remember my thumbnail worn down from steady use. But let's face it. No more vacant lots or dusty driveways. And what about pocketknives, Mumbelty Peg, and tops?

(And while I'm on the subject, what ever happened to supper?)

It would appear, as a grandparent, that sex education is less complicated today than way back then. A click-click on the dot-com, and there it is, in color. The mystery was better—discovery and all that. Remember the day in high school when all the girls were herded into the auditorium and at the same time all the boys into the gym? The coach talked to us about clean living and respect and natural changes and all that. We listened and wondered what this was all about and why were they telling us this? I mean, hadn't our Scoutmaster sort of said the same thing?

What was the school nurse telling the girls? Simply, they said something about growing up. Punctuation, periods, and other things. Wow!

Well, back to Kick-the-Can and hiding behind the garage with Vivian. Olley Olley Oxen Free! And supper's ready!

Chapter 9
Billy and the Perils of Pacific Grove

Back in the '30s when we lived in Kernville—I must have been seven or eight—I was climbing around a big pile of lumber across the ditch and found a mother cat with a half-dozen kittens, all yellow. I scooped them up in two or three trips and got them to our back porch. There they stayed, grew, and multiplied, until at one time we had close to thirty cats underfoot, all yellow, except one gray with a bobbed tail.

On one of our trips to Pacific Grove we took along one of the long-haired cats for Cousin Rose, Aunt Flora's cousin who lived in the Cottage. She named him Billy, and he was her closest pal until she died a few years later. Billy then became part of our family since we had moved to Pacific Grove permanently in 1941.

Somewhere along the line Dad decided it was a good idea to castrate Billy. He got Brooks and me to hold the cat, head down, in a gunnysack. He laid out his tools—a razor blade, fingernail scissors, and a bottle of Hexol, ready to do the job. Billy was pissed off in general at the preparations, not knowing what was about to happen, but pissed off just the same. He bit Brooks right through the gunnysack, and Brooks, now even more upset than Billy, started to cry and retired to the house to be comforted by Mom.

Dad then shoved the gunnysack, Billy still head down, into a rubber boot. With me watching closely, in case I ever had to do this, he slit the scrotum with a new Gillette Blue Blade (double-edged), held the nuts between two fingers, and finished off the job with the fingernail scissors. The noise from the boot was considerable, especially when Dad poured on the Hexol. Then out of the boot, out of the sack, Billy scooted to the end of the garage, hid for a few minutes, licked off the Hexol, and lived happily ever after. Well, not quite.

Many years later Billy had fallen on hard times, scarred from neighborhood fights, skinny and ratty-looking from old age. He smelled bad too. With the agreement of the family, Dad decided it was time to put old Billy to sleep. We had thought he might just wander off and die, but no such luck. Dad got a bottle of chloroform from Clyde Dyke down at the Grove Pharmacy and, from behind the soda fountain, an empty five-gallon malted milk can with a screw top.

In went a rag, then the chloroform, and then Billy, head first. Dad screwed the top on tight, Billy raising hell inside the can. It was a sad time—seemed like half an hour—as the bumping inside the can got slower and slower. Finally, no more bumps, and Dad unscrewed the top. Billy came out of that can, at least five feet, straight up, and headed east without even touching the ground.

He disappeared and stayed gone for at least two weeks. Then one afternoon, he came meowing at the back door as if nothing had happened. He looked pretty good, maybe a little skinny, and lived happily for two or three more years. Then he went to sleep in the laundry room one night and quietly passed away, all lives used up. We buried him back by the berry bushes. Dad thought maybe the chloroform had done him some good.

Chapter 10
Saved Again!

I suspect that one of the many reasons I'm such a fine person today is that growing up I went to church camp, at least every summer and sometimes in between. And the same for my kids, of course, and now, my grandkids. We did have weekend retreats and Christian campouts at Big Sur, but the *real thing* was a week or so at Mount Hermon and, not too far away, in the hills behind Aptos, Monte Toyon. My son Scott got to go to Young Life Malibu Club in British Columbia. Check that one out on the Internet and realize that if you can't find Christ there, you're hopeless! Matter of fact, Scott went there twice.

I bring this up since sitting in church today I happily daydreamed about the first time I was saved, and looking at the state of the nation I think a few more church camps might help our troubled youth. Couldn't hurt, at any rate.

Now church camps are not all Bible study, prayer, and salvation. From Mount Hermon there were trips to the beach, the Boardwalk, and nature hikes through the Santa Cruz Mountains. The leaders of these camps realized that fatigue is the best chaperone, but it seemed that the leaders were usually exhausted before the campers. These camps, of course, were boys and girls together, and love, puppy or otherwise, is a very Christian thing. Emotions became more intense as the campers matured, but nobody could get in real trouble in one week! Fear of eternal damnation, shame in the eyes of Jesus, and the Ten Commandments usually kept ardor safely fluttering in the chest. Oh, I'm sure a time or two a kiss was stolen behind a redwood or deep in the ferns, but after all, God is love! There was, indeed, the time a young man of my acquaintance came home from Malibu with mono, known in those days as the "kissing disease." A later letter from a lovely redhead in Dallas confirmed the coincidence of her coming down with the same virus.

During the spiritual discussions, late at night in the boys' tent, it came up more than once that our Catholic contemporaries could sin to their heart's content, and then confess it all on Saturday. But then we agreed that sin of a sort can be delicious thing and would be no fun at all without a little guilt.

We were blessed at church camp with marvelous speakers and preachers who coaxed us into public confessions and flowery but sincere "witness." Earlier I recalled the first time I was saved, but I think that all of us were saved again and again at every church camp. By the end of the week emotion and fervor were so intense we couldn't refuse, and after all, we knew it couldn't hurt!

My brother Mike recalls our mother's admonition as he left for his first church camp. "Mike," she said. "Don't make promises you can't keep." Now I'm not sure how that fits with salvation, but it was nevertheless good advice and has stuck with him these many years later. Promises to the Lord are not to be made lightly.

One of the high points was a presentation by a fine evangelist who said, "I'm going to show you something you haven't seen before, and after you see it, you'll never see it again!" Well, the guy pulls out of his pocket a *peanut*, cracks the shell, shows us the nut, then *eats* it! The religious significance is a touch obtuse, but it's there, if you work on it. This act was also effective in entertaining Cub Scouts later in life.

If I remember right, another high point was the campfire where we recited a verse and then tossed a "faggot" on the fire. The faggot was a short piece of wood, and the verses were pretty short, too. (Jesus wept.)

Music was always a big part of church camp. We belted out our old favorites—"Christ for Me," "I've Got the Joy, Joy, Joy, Joy Down in My Heart," and even "Jesus Loves Me." Thankfully this was all before "Kumbaya" or rap.

On the last night, holding hands around the fire, we promised to love and serve the Lord, and indeed we have. Then home to showers and pleased parents, and on the following Sunday at Mayflower Congregational Church, we witnessed.

Saved again, and comforting to know that I still am! Amen.

Chapter 11
Gabriel, Revisited

All cities, towns, and villages have their own sets of sounds. Not like a thumbprint, exactly, but when you woke up in the morning and heard the soft, sonorous sibilance of the surf, or the low moaning of the foghorn or the bell buoy, you remembered that you were back home in PG. In Monterey it was the gulls, and in the good old days, the cannery whistles. In Carmel, of course, the Mission and Monastery bells on Sunday morn.

This was all well and good, but without some *punctuation* you might have thought yourself in Santa Cruz or Santa Clara. Our punctuation in PG was THE FIRE HORN! Mounted on top of City Hall, which was also the Fire Station in those days of yesteryear, it was part of our identity, our heritage, and our signature sound, unlike anything else in Western civilization. It was harsh and raucous, insistent and serious in intent. Its primary purpose was to alert and call the volunteer firemen, day or night, rain or shine, war and peace. During World War II it called us all to air raid and/or blackout drills, and that, indeed, is another story.

Noon, every day, was announced with two blasts—"Twelve o'clock, Nellie! We've made it through another day!" It was always exciting for out-of-town guests to hear it for the first time. We proudly suggested it was part of our New England heritage. Some thought it woke the dead and killed the living. Not true, of course, but I'll tell you this: damn few pigeons stayed on City Hall.

It must be recalled that in those days the Rec Center, high school hangout, was on Forest Avenue, right across from City Hall. One moonlit night a friend of mine was dancing—"String of Pearls"—with a pretty little honey from Chowchilla, sweet sixteen and all the rest. (No really, never been.) They stepped outside for a breath of air, and he, also never, asked if he could kiss her. Unable to speak, she nodded yes, and as he planted his lips to hers, the horn, maybe fifty feet away, and heard fifty miles away, blew! At first, trembling in his awkward grasp, she thought that *sound*, which indeed did shake her teeth, was part of the kissing experience. At second and third blast, however—there was a house fire down by Caledonia—she realized this was GOD! She burst into tears and did not kiss again until her freshman year at San Jose State.

The horn has long since gone, having served us well those many years. My brother Brooks was an eager volunteer, later to become a "regular." We lived at 18th and Laurel, and on that corner the horn was practically in our bedroom. Brooks kept his turnout gear, boots and all, by his bed, and when the horn blew in the middle of the night, he hit the deck, boots on, and ran full blast to the station. Don Gasperson, retired Chief, tells me that they needed three volunteers before they could roll the truck, and I'll bet Brooks was at least number two. Don also tells of being on duty alone at night, sound asleep, and when a box was pulled sending in an alarm, all the lights in the station (now on Pine), the horn, bells, and sirens went off at once. He might have wondered if he wanted to do this for the rest of his life. Good for us he did! Back in the '40s he worked at Johannsen's Creamery, down Forest, just below Lighthouse, and when he heard the blast, middle of root beer float or not, he was over the counter and up the hill. And by golly, he's still in good shape. Oh well, a new hip, but what would you expect, sliding down a brass pole for thirty-seven years.

I grew up as a fireman's kid. My dad was a Forest Ranger in Kernville, Bakersfield, and San Luis Obispo, and later Chief at the Line School—now Navy Postgraduate—and then the Presidio.

Six years old, San Luis Obispo. I could hear the siren coming from down the street. Playing in the front yard, and there it came! Red, shiny, open-cab fire truck, probably a La France, and the siren louder than ever. And there, in the driver's seat, all by himself, was my daddy! He waved and grinned, and away he went. I stood there, transfixed, for a few seconds, then ran into the house. "Mama, Mama! Daddy just went by in the fire truck!" She smiled, and she said, "Oh boy!"

The horn was part of the fine volunteer tradition in Pacific Grove. We all had posted in our homes the code telling the approximate location of the fire. "One, One, Three," Forest and Lighthouse, and there was a chalkboard in front of the station with the address of the blaze.

Most of us are pulled to witness the drama of a fire, even firemen off duty. My dad and Brooks were first out the door, followed by me, Mike, Shirley, and Tom, Dad calling "Let's see if they can save the lot!" (Fireman humor.) Often false alarms, but the two world-class blazes, PG High School and the Grove Theater, were never to be forgotten. Then there was our High School Pep Rally bonfires at the east end of the football field—torched one night early by a wily pyromaniac, but built bigger and better the next night. Roll, Breakers, Roll! Pyromaniac was sneaking up with a bow and arrow to do it again, just like the Indians, but caught in the act, he ran away! (I'll never tell, John.)

There has to be a certain calling to be a fireman, volunteer or regular. Sure, it's exciting, dramatic, romantic, and most of all rewarding, but it's also often dirty, dangerous, and backbreaking hard work. Just try pulling those charged hoses around! And then, after the fire is out, the cleanup, washing the hoses, and getting everything ready for the next alarm. When those guys and gals go by in the next Good Old Days parade, give them an extra cheer and a real "thanks" when you walk by the station.

Now, I suppose, cell phones call the "Laddies" to come save the town. More efficient, I suppose, than the horn, and the chimes from City Hall will tell you when it's noon. But what about the girls from Chowchilla? Well, that's also another story.

Chapter 12
Aloha, or Big Time at the Royal Hawaiian

You won't remember Don Winslow unless you are on the north side of seventy, but let me tell you, Midshipman Winslow cut a fine figure in his dress uniform, sailing on the high seas, romantic foreign ports and high adventure. He was, of course, a hero of the comics, the "funny books," right along with Flash Gordon and Captain Midnight.

I think it might have been the vision of Don Winslow that pulled me toward the Navy, and into the NROTC, a midshipman indeed! Many adventures and stories were to follow, but the summer cruise, 1948, on the Battleship Iowa, was the capper, the pinnacle, and to an eighteen- year-old kid from Pacific Grove, *really* something!

I'll tell you later about the sixteen-inch guns, the sinking of the radioactive USS Nevada, sea snakes in the latrine, and my seasick shipmates, but for now. . .

The USS Iowa pulling in to Pearl Harbor was a *big deal!* For most of us, this was our first trip to Hawaii, and it seemed that everybody there was glad to see us. Navy band, hula girls on the dock, the smell of fuel oil and plumeria, and the promise of "dreams come true in Blue Hawaii," whatever that meant. It had to be better than Seattle!

After much spit and polish, and in our dress uniforms— remember Don Winslow?—we were off to a special dance at the OFFICER'S CLUB! Most of the young honeys in Honolulu (invitation only) were there, smiling, laughing, loaded with Hawaiian charm. My fraternity brother Bob Nelson and I, both very handsome and right out of central casting, tied up, so to speak, with two lovelies, the Walton sisters. (Not to be confused with the later TV series.) We danced, drank punch, and suaved away an hour or two, and then the girls, who were staying at THE ROYAL HAWAIIAN!, suggested that it would be nice if we took them home, dropped them off, said good night, and all that. Well!

Taxi from Pearl to Waikiki is a *very* long ride, and Bob and I had just enough to cover the fare with just enough, we hoped, to get us back to the ship without walking. No matter, romance was in the air!

We swept into the Royal Hawaiian, out onto the veranda, and oh my goodness there was the Hawaiian moon, the gentle surf, plumeria without the fuel oil, Harry Owens orchestra. . . what fine figures we cut! Two handsome midshipmen, two beautiful girls, dressed like a million bucks, and a dance or two. Then disaster struck.

One of the girls, the one on my arm as I recall, suggested *a bite to eat,* and *maybe something to drink!* Full speed ahead, again, and damn the consequences! We sat at the best table on deck, and the girls started to order. Some of this, and some of that, and don't forget the shrimp and lobster. And how about Mai Tais! Wonderful food, but I don't remember tasting any of it. We were doomed to disgrace, ridicule, and maybe even the brig. No matter if the tab was five or fifty, we knew there was a limit to Hawaiian hospitality, and oh my God, we had to get back to the ship! I knew we had to throw ourselves on the mercy of the establishment, and hopefully out of range of the gals.

It was understood that I would do the talking, glib and all that, and I beckoned to the waiter, who just smiled and walked away! There was a ten-minute pause, and desperation began to drip down my arms, through my splendid uniform. Finally, I explained to the girls that we just had to settle and leave or be confined to the ship for the rest of the summer and could they help us get the attention of the waiter so that we could shettle, I mean *settle*, the GODDAMN BILL! They could tell I was nervous.

And then, and then… they began to giggle and told us that it was all *compliments of the house! The Royal Hawaiian,* by God! Their *father* was President of the hotel. Not only that, they had a car at their disposal and drove us back to Pearl!

The next night, the one who had hung on the arm of Nelson invited him to a swish party at the hotel, but I suspect that since I swore out loud on the veranda, I was not included. But that was okay. The night of the party some of my shipmates and I parked our clothes behind a bowling alley on Waikiki and swam, out of sight, past the Outrigger, the Royal Hawaiian, and back. Now how many of you have done *that*!

Oh, and one more thing. Back to our clothes, still intact, but our wallets had been stripped of whatever pathetic cash we had. Not to worry! I had five bucks in a hidden pocket, and into Trader Vic's we went for fried bananas before heading back to the ship.

Aloha!

I almost forgot. The square in the Golden Gateway in San Francisco is named after the girl's father. You could look it up!

Chapter 13
Remember Pearl Harbor

Remember what? I could show you exactly where I was standing that Sunday morning when I first heard of Pearl Harbor. Just ten feet from where three years later I broke my arm. Eleven years old and didn't know Pearl Harbor from Cabo San Lucas, but from that moment on—well, you know the story. The date is now elusive, but I think in the previous year we sat in the PG Grammar School auditorium with a big radio on the stage, and listened to President Roosevelt tell us about all the planes, ships, and tanks we were going to build. We then knew the Germans and Japanese were all bad guys, and we had heard about war (England, China, and all that), but here we were, really *in* one, and boy, was that exciting! Maybe you don't remember Eagle Squadron and Yanks in the RAF, but that was *us*!

The gravity of it all slowly hit us, but still exciting, with Monterey Peninsula right in the thick of things. Fort Ord was alive with soldiers, coming and going, the boom of artillery night and day and the rifle ranges, right there, across the train tracks! Caissons went rolling along, part of convoys of trucks and armored vehicles, soldiers waving, bands playing, flags and banners flying, all part of the thrill. And the Presidio crackled with activity, with draftees and recruits being processed for war. Cavalry still had horses and mules, and machine gun practice up on the hill behind PG.

Old Del Monte Hotel became Navy Pre Flight with three or four football fields on the Polo Grounds and some of the best teams in the country. It was serious stuff as the boys left Pre Flight for Pensacola and elsewhere and came back pilots flying torpedo planes, dive bombers, and fighters over the bay. True or not, we thrilled at the story of Buzz Sawyer flying his Hell Cat *under* Bixby Bridge. And then that tragic crash of a torpedo plane out on Lighthouse, just missing that mansion that later was featured in *A Summer Place.* We had seen the plane flying low, then heard the crash. We ran all the way from the high school and watched as the Navy and our fire crews cleaned up.

The crew was killed, and the war didn't seem quite so much fun after that.

Early in the war we went through blackouts and air raid drills, marching out of the grammar school to the safety of the trees fifty yards away. If we ever got complacent—not likely—there were plenty of rumors to whip us up. KDON one night reported the possibility, actually the *likelihood,* that the Japanese were landing on the Santa Cruz Pier. That's right! Next to the Boardwalk! Silly now, but serious then. And if this was confirmed, we were to crack the blocks on our automobile engines, thereby denying the invaders access to the hinterland. Not taking any chances, some patriots with sledgehammers in hand cracked the blocks prematurely, thereby denying themselves transportation until after the war! Lucky we still had the Del Monte Express.

Speaking of transportation, gasoline was rationed along with tires, and other automobile parts were very hard to get. Not to be denied the joy of driving, some of the guys in auto shop built a sort of a car out of old salvaged parts. To accommodate the four sizes of worn and salvaged tires, each wheel was a different size. It was quite a sight to see the "shopmobile" hopping down the street with three or four grinning mechanics enjoying the ride. And once tasted, friends, you will never siphon gasoline again, $4 a gallon or not.

We were stunned when our Japanese classmates were moved away, and this even happened to some families of Italian descent, albeit for a brief period of time. Then, of course, there was the story of the German typewriter repairman discovered under the Salinas River bridge, transmitting "classified information" to God knows who.

One moonlit night, deep into a blackout, we stood outside wondering if this was a drill or the real thing. One of our neighbors didn't bother wondering, and having made a good dent in a fifth of Four Roses, he aimed and fired his .22, suspecting that the moon was the enemy. Missed the moon, but hit the clock on City Hall. He cracked the glass, but time marched on, and the glass was replaced after the war.

Families came and went, stationed here briefly, then away to some distant shore. Just about the time we developed a crush, they left, always promising to write. We bought Savings Bond stamps with our paper route money and grew great Victory Gardens. Boy Scout Troop 46, under the direction of Master Gardener Wilfred Mack, raised bushels and bushels of Idaho potatoes on the corner of Del Monte and Bayview, PG. Picture in the paper and all that. We learned first aid, collected fat cans, aluminum pots and pans, paper, and tires. We collected Army and Air Force shoulder insignia and any other military souvenir we could lay our hands on. (If you have forgotten what they looked like, log on to World War II military insignia, and get a lump in your throat.) Our moms cooked around the shortages and rations, and we ate a lot of fish. I don't remember thinking about it, but the Depression was over.

You may have seen that article in *Reader's Digest,* late 1945 or so, after the shooting was over. "Nostalgia for War," it said, longing again for the national unity, all of us on the same mission, same page, devoted to the same purpose, saving our country and the rest of the world. All well and good, but don't miss *Flags of Our Fathers.* And haven't you noticed? Our current war isn't quite the same.

Chapter 14
Heart of My Heart

Yes indeed, our friends were *truer* then, or maybe it was *dearer* then, but at any rate, the summer of '49 was glorious and it was fun to be alive! As Tom Wolfe said once upon a time, "Ah, to be drunk and twenty, and know that you will never die."

This was the summer I came home in minor disgrace, having flunked out of school, but none of my friends had distinguished themselves academically. I had a good set of credentials having been *away* to New Mexico, Juarez, Seattle, and Honolulu. To kids locked up by circumstance in Monterey County, that all seemed pretty grand. Oh, a few had gone as far away as San Jose, Santa Clara, or Berkeley, with a side trip to The City, but I could bullshit to my heart's content and nobody knew the difference. Of course, a slight brush with Keats, Shelley, and Byron didn't hurt either.

We all had decent jobs, a little money in our pockets, with nights of beer and guiltless sin. Boys and girls together, me and Mamie O'Rourke, we tripped the light fantastic on the sidewalks of Pacific Grove! It was a summer of recreational romance, old sweethearts for the weekend, memories and laughs of the Senior Dance, and those silly sock hops in the gym! But oh, they didn't seem silly at the time. We had been awash with anticipation of whatever, and of any innocence left to be betrayed.

We played cards in kitchens when parents didn't mind, and when they did, we got a cheap room at Lemos' Motel. We sang in between hands: "I like Torrelli, I like him very fine, I like Torrelli, I like him for his wine. Torrelli has my money, his wine is in my belly. If it were not for his wine, I would not like Torrelli!" And on and on.

One nice August night we were playing poker in Donna Miller's kitchen, across from the museum, just below Ruby's Soda Fountain. Donna, pretty and cute, was a lot of fun, as the saying goes, and particularly good at lip-synching records. "Come on-a my house, my house a-come on!" into the night.

On this particular night the air was blue with smoke, the beer cold, and the cards hot, but not hot enough. I looked across the table at Dusty, and Dusty looked across the table at me.

I don't think Dusty could lip-synch, but you only need one of those in the crowd anyway.

But Dusty was, and I'll bet still is, a very special gal. Tall, blond, long legs, blue eyes, "lips like cherries," tasted of peaches and cream, a throaty laugh, a big smile, and lots of fun to be with.

Dusty and I had lost interest in cards. Then she gave me that shy smile, and then, there came that "look," the look that I'll never forget. It was a look filled with promise of excitement, and I suppose, latent lust. There was a touch of foam from her can of Pabst on her upper lip. She could have wiped it off with her sleeve, but oh, sweet Jesus! She flicked it off with her tongue! Her look said very clearly that *tonight* we were going to *do it*.

Just in case you wonder, I was not, at this stage of my life, celibate, but almost. But that's not the point.

We left our cards on the table, and without saying goodbye, we stood up and walked out into the fog. A tentative hug, a kiss, then we touched each other's hair, a little damp already from the fog. We hopped into the car and drove away.

Ah, the *look*, I'll never forget. And if these many years later I bump into Dusty, say at Safeway, I'll ask her to just give me that look one more time.

Chapter 15
Del Monte Express

With all the wonderful things we have on the Monterey Peninsula, there's something missing: train sounds, and especially, train whistles. As recently as 1971 you could still hear the Del Monte Express moaning in and out of town, and if you can't remember that, rent the movie *Picnic*. (Not our whistle, but close enough.) If that doesn't work, for you there are lots of Web sites that will blow your horn.

When we lived in the East Bay, nighttime train sounds, in between a few gunshots, lulled us to sleep, or maybe even woke us up. It was all part of our world. Here in God's Country, we were blessed with mix of train whistles, foghorns, and bell buoys, and we slept the sleep of the innocents.

In PG the Del Monte was the railroad crown jewel, spending the night by Lover's Point. The track extended by our classic depot, out through the woods, past Asilomar to the Sand Plant where Spanish Bay now sprawls. That toot-toot-toot as the engine pulled hopper cars though the woods seemed just the right touch. Didn't seem to bother the butterflies, either. My train historians Jim and Rita deLorimier tell me that some kids really did hitch rides through the pines. The depot, painted that good old railroad tan, looked just like that model you might have made for your Lionel layout. The turntable was just beyond the depot and about fifty yards away, where we looked for golf balls, next to a very authentic outhouse. The lumberyard was on the other side of the depot with its own siding. One of the reasons I'm so strong today, sixty years later, is that I spent a couple of weeks unloading wet redwood from a flat car.

And wasn't it the Del Monte that collided with Doc Ricketts?

The Del Monte, in our heyday, pulled five or six passenger cars, with Oliver's Lounge car the back porch at the end. Oliver, who might have been a Pullman porter in earlier days, resplendent in a white starched jacket, served cocktails to contented passengers, home from a day marching around Union Square. Of course the bar closed before the Pacific Grove city line!

The train left PG at 7:00 sharp, with brief stops in Monterey, Del Monte, Fort Ord, and on to Castroville and points north, arriving at 3rd and Townsend in San Francisco at 10:00. Plenty of time for lunch at the Palace, St. Francis ("Meet you under The Clock"), the Fly Trap, or Bernstein's Fish Grotto. Spend a few bucks at the White House, back on the train at 4:00, and home in PG by 7:00!

Aside from the Del Monte, there was a lot of railroad here. Sidings up and down the line, big business on Cannery Row with tin shipped in for sardine cans, and cans of fish and fish by-products shipped out. Cement and lumber came and went, and Fort Ord was HUGE with tracks all over the place. The Y at Castroville carried trains south, picking up produce for the rest of the world in Salinas. DeLorimier's Monterey Bay Packing in Castroville shipped in all directions, taking advantage of both legs of the Y.

The Greyhound was our bridge to the main line in Salinas where we hopped aboard the Daylight, or the Starlight, or the Owl. And speaking of the Greyhound, remember when the end of the line—or the beginning of the line—was right there in downtown

PG at the corner of 17th and Lighthouse? Made it pretty easy to get out of town, not that anybody really wanted to.

When was the last time you rode a Greyhound, or a Trailways? A little primitive, perhaps, and maybe a little bumpy, but you met some very interesting people. It's a long time from here to Bakersfield, but plenty of stops along the way. I imagine that sounds pretty good when you fly coach to hither and yon.

Around 1950 my brother Brooks and I boarded the Daylight in Salinas and changed to the Chief in Los Angeles. Both trains were loaded with college kids headed back to school. A wonderful night on the Chief—you fill in the blanks—then off in Albuquerque for another year of serious study.

If you're retired and your schedule is loose, take the Amtrak north. Portland, Seattle, even Sacramento. The food is great, the scenery almost like it used to be, and there's a nice club car. I don't think there's a security check, and you don't have to take off your shoes. You can even walk around. Takes a little longer than Southwest, but what's the rush?

Every year we hear about a new committee, or study group, promising a new, if shorter, Del Monte. Don't count on it, friends. But Salinas really isn't that far away and I think they're going to paint the station!

As the sign said in the old days, *Next Time Try the Train*!

Chapter 16
Happy Valentine's Day!

Oh Valentine, my Valentine!
Be my sweetie Valentine!

Valentine's Day was always a day of romance and promise, sincere or otherwise, but never more so than in the fourth grade at Horace Mann in Bakersfield. The day when you would know if she really liked you, might even say she *loved* you, and you could indicate the same. We wouldn't even have to sign the cards, but we would *know*! This was all before sex was invented, but there was still some wonderful shortness of breath, a fluttering in the chest, just knowing that you might be able to stand next to her in the cafeteria line. I suspect even our teacher, Miss Cartwright, thought she might get some recognition of affection—*finally*—from someone other than her pupils.

The class was all caught in the same dippy frenzy, making lists, cutting out hearts and flowers, and even buying some at the dime store for a penny apiece. I just couldn't cut hearts— always lopsided—so mine came from the store, but very carefully selected.

Miss Cartwright let some of the more artistic kids make the Valentine Box, about two feet square and deep, with a slot on top, the whole thing dressed with hearts, doily paper, and cutouts of cupids and arrows. As a finishing touch they pasted on those tiny candy hearts, the ones with the messages like "Hot Stuff," "Oh You Kid," "Me Too," and "Be Mine."

The box began to fill about two weeks ahead. Miss Cartwright smiled a wan smile as the offerings dropped, knowing that she had to endure this, knowing that with twenty-eight kids in the class there would be at least twenty-eight envelopes addressed to her. And knowing this, as she had for the past seven years, she dropped in twenty-eight cards, each with the same inane message, knowing that they would all be compared. The girls sent cards to each other, and maybe two or three to certain boys. We boys mostly favored girls, and those of us with early political instincts included all of them. To other boys, we sent those mildly insulting or comic cards, and of course there was always two or three "naughty" or obscene ones. At any rate, the box filled to the brim, and last period on Valentine's Day, off came the lid and the chosen few girls handled the distribution. Being one of the "certain boys," my stack grew early and I noticed that Amy Custer's stack was growing pretty fast, too. I was pleased to see that my offering to her had been set somewhat aside where it might attract the most attention.

Leila Jackson, notably unpopular, was receiving more than some of the better-liked girls, and it was loudly whispered that she had sent several to herself! As the monitors danced up and down the aisles like little cupids, Miss Cartwright passed out pink-frosted heart-shaped cookies she had made the night before. All was well, and we looked forward to studying our cards at home, comparing them with friends, exaggerating the count when necessary. The box was empty, smiles around the room.

As we all glanced around, seeing who got what, William Bagley, sitting in the back corner of the room, was quietly looking out the window, maybe just a touch of tear on his cheek. William was not popular, and worse, he was one of the kids who were just plain ignored. Neither liked nor disliked, he just wasn't noticed. We couldn't remember when he arrived at our school or where he lived, or anything about him. A few freckles, reddish hair, clothes maybe a little different, but all in all, he just wasn't there. And of course, the only Valentine on his desk, with his hand over it, was the one from the teacher.

There were embarrassed whispers—no giggles—and then, quiet. Miss Cartwright hadn't noticed.

"All right, children. Everyone back to their seats."

But up stood Amy. She took a Valentine off her pile and walked to William's desk. Miss Cartwright started to say something, but thought better of it.

"Here, William," said Amy. "I got too many, and I think some of these got mixed up."

William looked at her, started to smile, and by golly, there *was* a little tear on his cheek. He tried to say something, but nothing came out. He nodded and looked down on her card, placed on top of the teacher's.

Amy smiled, look straight ahead, and walked back to her desk. And then Doris, who really didn't have too many of her own, took the biggest one off her pile, and without saying a word, walked back and put it on William's desk. No words were necessary.

Not to be left out, every girl in the class, even Leila, did the same. William really didn't know what to do, but with quiet grace accepted these tokens of friendship. Miss Cartwright knew that something special was happening and said nothing.

Blessedly, blessedly the bell rang, and Valentine's Day was over.

And what about William? Well, he did just fine. The next day at school the kids in the class all said "Hi, William" and made no mention of the previous day, but he was recognized and noticed from then on. He moved away at the end of the year, a happier kid than when he arrived at Horace Mann.

And oh, yes. Amy. In the sixth grade, she did tell me that she loved me. Even gave me a flashlight for my birthday. Now how about that!

Chapter 17
The Day I Wet My Pants (In School)

If you've never wet your pants, which I seriously doubt, the following might not be fully appreciated. There is something fixed firmly in memory about the sensation of warm liquid running down the inside of your leg, past the knee, and into your sock. . . and how quickly it turns cold. Well, enough of sodden recollection. I blame this incident not on lack of self-control, but rather on some viral condition or possibly an early injury sustained from pissing on an electric fence.

I was in the seventh grade, probably eleven years old, at the Pacific Grove Grammar School. It all started in woodshop, where I was one of two tool room monitors. This was a highly sought-after responsibility, bestowed on those most favored by the shop teacher, Mr. Lebec. The first accident—yes, more to follow—was just that, and although I can't remember the details, I suspect I finished too quickly before class and in a rush to beat the bell, dampened my corduroys. No great tragedy in itself, but still, not anxious to call attention to this mishap, I hustled around the tool room, and ohmygod, ripped the side of my pants on a saw—a ripsaw—and thereby exposed my briefs. This was noticed, of course, by the other monitor, who called it to the attention of Mr. Lebec. I was rendered somewhat speechless but did mumble that I might go home and change. Mr. Lebec had a better idea! The girls' sewing class was in the room next to the woodshop; why not get Mrs. Parker, the teacher, to come whipstitch the rip and save the day! And in she came, with needle and thread, as I was about to faint. I prayed to God that she wouldn't notice the damp, and if she did she didn't wet on. I mean, let on. She smiled her teacher-smile and went back to class. I'm sure she kept the confidence. The bell rang, and saved I was! No, not quite.

I was off to English class, where I sat in the back of the room, blessedly next to the radiator, which I knew would dry my cords and all would be well. Then *horrors*! The teacher, Miss Cline, announced a spelling contest—fun, fun, fun—right side of the room against the left, and to stand in from of the room and read the words, *ME*! Death was not far away, but the worst was yet to come. I stood in front of the class as close to the front desk as I could, hiding, I hoped, any damp, and began to read the words. Yes, correct, no, incorrect, etc. All going well, and then, my God! I had to pee! Nerves, nerves, nerves. My shattered mind prayed for help, but could I, standing in front of the class, ask the teacher to be excused to go to the *bathroom*? I prayed for a fire drill, an earthquake, a baseball through a window—anything!

The only thing to do was to let just a little go, and no one would notice. In this state of panic I said "Correct" to a couple of wrong words, howls from the class. I couldn't have cared less. The bell rang and I tried to muddle the puddle by my feet, with limited success, threw down the speller, ran home, changed pants and rushed back to school, a wreck for the rest of the week.

The miracle of it all: no one, teacher or classmate, ever knew of, or least mentioned, my personal disaster. The only aftereffect might have been a few months' delay in puberty. God is indeed good to the young and righteous.

Chapter 18
Primal Instinct

Tom, the kid next door, came home one afternoon with a bloody nose. Blood, anyway, down his new white shirt. Knowing him as a nice, peaceful sort of kid, I was surprised and asked what happened. As he told me, with a half-grin on his flushed face, boy, did the years fold back! The class bully, showing off, pulled Tom's hair and called him a sissy. The hair pull did it, and with rage beyond all fear or reason, Tom tore into the bully, shouting at the top of his lungs, flailing, kicking, determined to maim or kill his tormentor. The bully started to laugh, but when Tom landed a lucky shot to his nose he began to fear for his life and started to back away and, finally, run. His fear was by then greater than Tom's rage, and he was soon out of range of further mayhem. Tom shook and gasped for breath, but he knew that he had won his first real fight, and better yet, in front of the girls.

I remembered that eighth-grade afternoon, across the street from Pacific Grove Grammar School (now Robert Down), when sweet Mary Lou tangled with a tall, skinny gal recently arrived from Texas. We seemed to hear a frightening low growl, and then they flew at each other with a fury we had never seen before. It was *loud* with fistfuls of hair, ripped clothes, and torn lips. They were *pissed* and not a bit worried about survival. Finally, a teacher trotted across Pine Avenue and very bravely took charge.

Primal rage is a valuable gift that hides within all of us, unleashed without notice, triggered by a gross insult, usually physical. Fourth grade seems to be the threshold, and listening to Tom I was back in that mountain town schoolhouse with four grades and one teacher. One kid in my class was tall, redheaded, blue-eyed, and skinny. He had the unfortunate habit of wetting his pants, and I, even more unfortunately, thought this was funny. I might not have laughed out loud, but I certainly did snicker. And every day, after school, he would knock me down in the dusty street. My friends were on my side, but they also knew I was getting what I deserved.

After a week or two of this routine—I was a slow learner—he hit me on my nose. This was his mistake. A punch in the nose, like pulled hair, wipes away in an instant all fear, reason, and further pain. I stood up and charged, shouting whatever obscenities I knew, and went for his throat, face, ribs, and midsection. He was stunned by the attack and did his best to protect himself, but I got his nose, lip, and right eye, his glasses having flown into the dust on my first charge. Luckily our teacher arrived on the scene and took us, both sobbing, into the washroom for a cleanup. No lasting damage, and by later that afternoon we were good friends, playing Cowboys and Indians, both on the same side.

Fights of rage should not be confused with staged fights of honor, wherein scores were settled. PG High, around 1945, the word was out! McMann and Adams, both seniors, had decided to fight over sweet Jolene, who was maybe fifteen. Back behind the gym, she stood apart from the crowd, arms crossed, watching quietly as they took each other apart. After a few minutes, and plenty of blood, I think they both decided that maybe she wasn't worth it. They shook hands and walked into the gym together to clean up. Jolene walked home by herself, arms still crossed and wondering what it all meant.

We can all remember real rage moments, usually on the school grounds. Not to discount incidents of real courage or bravery, but Medal of Honor veterans have said that, more often than not, blind unthinking rage had pushed them through acts of heroism. Not the same as the schoolyard, but that deep, deep trigger waits to be pulled in us all.

Teachers and moms and dads are familiar with these tornadoes of temper, maybe having been there themselves, keeping their eyes open, especially with bullies around.

We can talk love and peace and common sense till the cows come home, but understand that primal, instinctive reaction sits quietly, waiting.

Chapter 19
Sex...

I tread lightly here, but in reconsidering those halcyon days of yesteryear, the '40s and '50s in Pacific Grove, I would be false to my memory if I didn't at least touch on the obsession with sex. This, of course, was healthy, normal, puzzling, and exciting, all at once. And dare I say that this obsession continues to this very day, even in Carmel! That great scholar, Page Smith, in a column a long time ago, said something to the effect that even at his advanced age at that time—probably late seventies or early eighties—the obsession was stronger than ever! I had the luck a few days ago to buy at a rummage sale some books from Eldon Dedini's collection, and you will note that Eldon turned this obsession into a very fine living and a place in history. Keep in mind that he was also a very devout Episcopalian.

You can only imagine the stir when the first issue of *Playboy* arrived in December of 1953 (and I might add that the most recent issue is not too bad either). Even those stout, devout Christians who ruled the roost in God's Hometown, Pacific Grove, recognized that every living one of us was the result of sex in one form or another. Actually, in one form, really, but let's not mess with Mother Nature.

To learn about this whole thing was difficult. There was always some smart-ass kid who claimed a certain knowledge and was willing to share his insights, lurid, fascinating, and false. And then there were the kids around the corner who played Doctor and may indeed have later gone to medical school. Moms and dads did their best to explain the mysteries, but seemed always to stop just an inch before the spread of pollen. Mr. Ferdinand Ruth, the world's best biology teacher, did his best to explain the mechanics, but always through discussion of other mammals, vertebrates, nonvertebrates, and sea urchins. But somehow we got the picture. Just look around. This leads me, of course, to "The Facts of Life, Circa 1938."

Chapter 20
The Facts of Life, Circa 1938

As I recall, my first exposure to the "facts of life" was in Kernville when I was in the third or fourth grade, or maybe in the summer in between. The instructor, so to speak, was Heidi Scheinholz, a classmate and friend who lived on the bluff right above the ranger station. Heidi was, and I suppose still is, a take-charge kind of girl, a matchmaker, organizer, and arbitrator. Her self-esteem and superior knowledge of most things never seemed to bother us. I suppose she was cute, and maybe still is, but that didn't occur to me at the time. The high point in our friendship, the following notwithstanding, was when she delivered to me the pink piece of scratch paper with "I love you" penciled in from Joanne Merganthaler, another classmate, who was indeed cute, sweet, shy, and quiet.

That summer my mother was seriously pregnant with brother Mike. This was of some note in Kernville where my dad, Ranger Bowhay, and his family were well-known and -liked. One afternoon Heidi asked me if I knew where babies came from. I don't remember my response, but whatever it was it didn't satisfy Heidi.

"Look," she said. "I do, and I'll tell you."

In the dust of the ranger station driveway she began to write out the answer to this mystery with a stick, one letter at a time. Since this was confidential information, she would rub out the letter as soon as I said that I had seen it. The problem was, about three or four letters into the procedure, I forgot what they were and she had to start all over again. This went on until dark and we were forced to postpone the revelation until the next day.

This time she agreed to write out a whole word before rubbing it out, but even this became difficult. Finally, with impatience that only a girl like Heidi could pull off, she said, "All_right! I'll spell the whole thing!" And she did, but there was a dramatic pause after each word, and frankly, I was beginning to lose interest. I mean, how important was this whole thing, anyway?

She wrote it down, in driveway dust, glancing up to make sure no one snuck up to see our secret, and finally, there it was: "The man puts his front end up to the woman's front end." What, I thought, does she mean by front end?

"Oh," I said. "I see." I really didn't see, and none of this made any sense. I mean, after all! Later, much later—years, in fact—I learned that there was more to the story. Alas, Heidi was, by then, long gone.

We spent the rest of the afternoon looking for turtles.

Chapter 21
Front!

Bing!

The desk clerk bangs the bell, says "Front!," and the bellhop steps up to take the guests and their luggage to their room. The Waldorf-Astoria? The Fairmont? The Saint Francis? No, the magnificent Forest Hill Hotel, pride of Pacific Grove, haven to traveling salesmen, retreat for movie stars, and employer of kids from Pacific Grove High School in the 1940s! The guests also included seasonal refugees from the Valley heat, wandering tourists, some retirees, and maybe even a trollop or two. You know it now, of course, as the Forest Hill Manor, still grand and snug, but certainly without any trollops. How nice it is now, maintained and enlarged.

In those old days the best jobs for kids, not to mention some adults, were at Holman's or the Hotel. At the Forest Hill we were hired only if the maroon and gray-striped uniforms fit, and if we were strong enough to carry four suitcases at a time. We were glorious to behold, with the badge of honor—a brass ring with the pass key attached—around our necks. Johnny was still calling for Philip Morris, and the only thing we lacked was the little cap.

The bellhops not only greeted the guests, but also ran the elevator (a state-of-the-art Otis, all manual), sifted the butts and spit out of the sand ashtrays, and ran whatever errands the front desk required. We got paid fifty cents an hour, plus tips, which ran from nothing to a buck or two.

There was me and my brother Brooks, Reg Murphy, Don and Dick and Len and Jerry and dozens more over the years. My sister Shirley waited table in the dining room. It was the best job I ever had, except for the last one. Handsome as we were, you might suspect an occasional romance with teenage guests, but the rules were strict. Nothing more than a pleasant smile. (Perhaps there *were* one or two minor exceptions. . . .)

Now and then we saw movie stars and other celebrities. Robert Young showed up with a reservation for a corner suite, a nice lady at his side. Flipped me his keys and told me to park his Chrysler Town & Country. Yessir, and I hopped in the driver's seat, but didn't know what in the hell to do next. The only starter I had ever seen was a big button on the floorboard. Nothing there! Nothing on the dash, or anyplace else. Finally, after a very long five minutes, I twisted the key in desperation, and the thing started! Keys back to his room, no tip yet, and he told me to bring him a fifth of Black & White scotch and a bottle of Dry Sack sherry. What to do? I explained that Pacific Grove was dry, but maybe Luther, the maintenance man, could run the errand. Gave Luther a twenty, and away he went up to Dode's, just outside PG. He returned with the booze, and scored five bucks. Two bucks for me, not to mention a twenty-yard ride in a T&C.

Other movie folks usually stayed at Pebble Beach, but little Natalie Wood, just a few months after her discovery with an ice cream cone, showed up with her parents. Natalie played Jean Tierney as a little girl in *The Ghost and Mrs. Muir* on location down the coast. After I did a short article about her for the local paper, she suggested I come to Hollywood as her press agent, but I felt I couldn't leave the hotel in the lurch. Oh, well.

The anchor guests were the "permanents" who rented suites at the ends of the floors. They were "high class," usually kind and generous. Miss Hilda Van Sicklen, whose father invented the speedometer (odometer?), was a charming philanthropist. You will recognize the well-intentioned but questionable bronze butterfly in Lover's Point Park, given to the city by her years ago. She also insured that my high school class won every war bond drive, somewhat discouraging to the others.

Uncle Jimmy Parke of Parke-Davis and Mrs. Parke moved in 1942 from their home, now the Martine House, into one of the front corner suites. He happily passed out pennies and cigar bands along with gracious smiles and conversation.

An old German gentleman, whose name escapes me, told me confidentially that "A rolling stone gathers no moss" and repeated this daily as he gave me a dime, gratefully received. Then there was the Scandinavian who claimed to be the first person to complete a ski jump inside Madison Square Garden. He was an erstwhile Olympic competitor whose skiing career ended when he tried to retrieve a bottle of whiskey dropped from a chair lift and broke his leg.

You can look at the Manor today and appreciate how good it must have looked in the old days. It was a center of the town. The spacious dining room, with diverse offerings, was home to Rotary, Lions, and Kiwanis, not to mention other locals who came for special Sunday dinners. There were parties and dances, all dry, of course. The view from the lobby was pleasant, from the front rooms upstairs, spectacular. The lobby itself had a homey sort of sophistication with wicker furniture, potted palms, brass ashtrays, and Oriental rugs, and it smelled of fine cigars. Strangely out of place in one corner of the west lounge was an electrolysis salon.

There was a rumor that bellhops, on quiet nights, rode on top of the elevator car, and even hunched under those giant springs at the bottom of the shaft, sometimes with impressionable girlfriends. How could anybody believe such a thing!

Rain or shine, as I remember, business was good. Maybe not a full house every night, but certainly enough to make it profitable, and there was still plenty of business for the inns and motels out in the woods. People really liked to visit Pacific Grove. There is the legend, of course, that the ghost of the venerable Mr. Parsons, the founder, with his high starched collar, still strolls through the lobby, checking the ashtrays.

Chapter 22
Take Your Girlie to the Movies

That was the first line of the old song that you might remember
if you are advanced enough in age. The next line is "If you can't
make love at home!" "There's no little brother there who always
squeals. You can say an awful lot in seven reels!" Okay, and you
won't remember that phrase "Pitch a little woo!" either.

Most of the time we walked down to the Grove Theater Saturday
afternoon, met our pals, bought our candy next door, then hustled
on in for a big dose of Captain Midnight, Movietone News, and
Buck Jones. Close your eyes for a minute, take a deep breath, and
you can just *smell* the place.

Then, as the lights went down, except for those stars in the
ceiling, we were enveloped in the *velvet dark*. The music swelled,
the huge red velvet curtain opened, and there we were, fascinated
PG kids, entranced and transported for a couple of glorious hours!
We dreamed of kissing sweet Doris Day, Jeanne Crain, Kathryn
Grayson, and Greer Garson. At least, I did!

We envied Errol Flynn, thought we might take up yachting
later in life. (Never did.) We shared adventure with Clark Gable,
Hopalong Cassidy, and John Wayne, and a little later in life
attempted to share adventure with some sweet lovely in the upper
loges. The loges were somewhat plush leather seats in the balcony.
They cost a little more, but were worth it if you were intent on
holding hands, or whatever. I must confess, reputation to the

contrary, that I never did "make out" in the balcony, but then I haven't been in the loges recently, either.

The Grove Theater was classy, both grand and intimate, and when it burned—a glorious fire!—we lost a big piece of our history, and maybe some of our future as well. (The feature that night was *The Toast of New Orleans*, with Mario Lanza.) The Golden State in Monterey, now wonderfully restored, did take up the slack, but it's not quite the same. I look now at the place right in front of the left balcony where I sat with sweet Marie and saw *Dumbo*. Hmm. Maybe it was sweet Annie, or could have been sweet Vivian. Whatever! Not a romantic epic, but at thirteen it was just right. Then a soda at Kips, and back to PG on the bus. Take your girlie to the movies, all right!

We all dreamed of being *in* the movies, not just in front of the screen, and one of us almost made it, or so the legend goes. Hollywood searched the state to find a kid just right for *The Yearling*. Remember the book? As the story goes, they found him in Pacific Grove! Yep, Ted Richmond. Bad luck struck, however, and the deer died, and Ted was aced out of a place in the movie magazines. I mean, better the deer than Ted! He went on, however, to star in basketball and golf.

(You can see his picture in the 1947 *Sea Urchin*, our class yearbook, holding a trophy.)

With Osio and Century at our doorstep, we see some pretty good flicks, thanks to Clint, but the theaters just don't smell the same. Better? Worse?

As a later line in the song cautioned, "When the picture's over and it's time to leave, Don't forget to brush the powder off your sleeve!"

No, I'm *sure* it was Marie.

Chapter 23
Waste Not

I should have learned, early in life, the folly of not following orders precisely, or just as bad, of trying to save friends and authorities from foolish mistakes. Not that I expected praise, or even compliments, from these altruistic actions. It was just that, with a Christian upbringing, there was the need to do *good* or avoid waste, or something like that. Then there was the added folly of thinking I knew better, was smarter than, etc., etc.

Let me give you an example. During my last year of active duty, I was stationed at a small but *very* important Navy station amongst the sloughs west of Vallejo. Skaggs Island, to be exact. Since it had a limited number of officers, I was Personnel Officer, Security Officer, *and* First Lieutenant (responsible for all spaces and equipment and anything else assigned by the CO). Well, it seems that at one time previous, probably during World War II, Skaggs was a training facility, and next to one of the Quonsets was a stack of once-upon-a-time beautiful antique oak tables, used in classrooms, and painted good old Navy gray. The Captain, wanting, naturally, a clean station, said, "Mr. Bowhay, we have no need of that lumber. Have it hauled out to the end of the island, and burned!"

I complied, but not until I had salvaged one of the least damaged, hauled it back to our quarters, and sanded and refinished it, restoring it to its previous glory. We used it as a dining table for years, and it now sits in the basement waiting for discovery by the next generation. That sort of success did embolden, and even though this minor disobedience was for my own benefit and not the Navy's, I felt there was no harm done, and as a matter of fact, still feel that way.

My next attempt to Waste Not was purely for the intended benefit of the Service and you, the Taxpayer. We had all heard of brand-new Jeeps, tanks, trucks, and airplanes being shoved over the side in the Pacific after the war, for any number of reasons. Such waste was not to happen on the watch of Lt. (JG) Bowhay!

There was furnished housing on the station for most of the personnel, and one of the by-products was a room full of slightly used double mattresses, top quality, Navy specs and so on, maybe twenty or so. Since the station budget called for *new* mattresses, the Skipper directed me to take old ones out to the edge of the station, and *burn them*! Certainly easy enough to comply, but these looked like pretty good mattresses, and smart-ass that I was, I got in touch with a mattress company in Vallejo. They agreed to take these twenty mattresses, and rebuild and restore and return to the U.S. Navy five *brand-new* mattresses *at no charge*! Now doesn't that seem like a sweet deal to you? Boy, did I catch hell! Not following orders, to begin with, and worse yet, f—ing with the system!

"Send those goddamn mattresses back!"

I did, and the mattress company was very pleased.

I think I saved my career when I found a brand-new, beautiful brass ship's clock that had somehow fallen out of inventory. I took it to the Captain, said I didn't know what to do with it. He happily said he would take care of it, and "Keep up the good work, Lieutentant (JG)."

Fearing a midnight call from the FBI, I took nothing with me when I was released from active duty, except, of course, the antique dining room table. I did find in my toolbox an old carpenter's wood clamp that may have fallen from inventory, like the ship's clock, but I just can't be sure.

Now apple falling close to the tree and all that, my dad had an even stronger aversion to waste than I. He dreamed of fortune from War Surplus, but never got beyond the dreaming stage. Once, almost, but not really.

At the time, he was Fire Chief at the old Hotel Del Monte, in service then as Navy Line School. The CO called him in one fine day and said, "Chief, I understand there are a hundred or so kapok life jackets, Building A-106-B. Never used, of course, but we need the space so get rid of them, burn 'em."

Not to argue, but imagine how this struck a thrifty taxpayer like my dad!

"Raymond," he said to one of the firemen just going off duty, "we've got to save those life jackets! Load them in your truck, put them in your garage, and we'll decide what to do with them later. Maybe give them to the Sea Scouts!"

Away Raymond went, happy to be of service to his country. Later that afternoon, oh my, came the word that maybe government property was missing and that Naval Intelligence, of all things, was investigating! Nothing specific about life jackets, but close enough. Dad got Raymond on the phone and told him, "Raymond, I don't care how you do it, but get rid of those life jackets!" I think he might have even mentioned prison.

Raymond, not too bright but earnest, complied. That night, along about midnight, he drove his truckload of life jackets out to the end of Wharf Number Two, dumped his cargo over the side, and drove home happily.

The next morning, not so happily, the CO called my dad.

"Bowhay!" he bellowed. "The goddamn Coast Guard just phoned, says there are life jackets all over Del Monte Beach! I don't know how it happened, and I don't *want* to know! Get those goddamn life jackets picked up *right now,* and give them to the goddamn Sea Scouts! Goodbye!"

Think of the terrible waste if those jackets had been burned. . . .

Chapter 24
The Unfairness of It All

Remember the unfairness of it all?

The teacher would pick two captains—later to become real athletes, jocks—to pick the sides. Flip a coin to see who goes first, then take turns choosing kids. Those already picked, of course, would give loud advice to their captain. So down the class it went, good athletes first, then the next tier, and on down to those poor wretches, always at the bottom. The logic, of course, was solid, with both sides somewhat balanced—a technique adopted in later years establishing expansion teams in baseball.

I say the process was unfair since I was always one or two from the bottom. I may have been good-looking, smart, and what have you, even a sometime pet of the teachers, but my athletic abilities didn't really surface until later, in high school. So maybe the process wasn't really unfair, but it did leave a few scars on the old self-esteem.

I was usually saved from the bottom by my best friend, Richard Stockton, who was even smarter than me, but he was also fat.

Richard's father was a prominent judge, and they lived in a beautiful house on a hill. Behind the house was vacant land, acres and acres, still part of the prairie. After school and on weekends we tramped around, finding trapdoor spiders, scorpions, and gopher snakes. We scratched out a cave and kept our treasures there and talked about the books were reading—*Tom Swift*, the Oz series, the Bobbsey Twins—and ate cookies from his mother's kitchen. We listened to *General Shafter Parker and His Circus* and *I Love a Mystery* with Jack, Doc, and Reggie. We had Orphan Annie Decoder Badges. Wrote messages in code. We were friends.

One afternoon in the spring we went through the "choosing" ritual for a softball game, and Richard and I were on the same side, at the bottom, of course. Lined up, we took our turns at bat, the teacher lobbing the ball across the plate. The other side got a run or two, but every time we got somebody on base, either Richard or I would strike out.

The kid behind me in line said to me in a quiet voice, "If it wasn't for *Fatso*, we might have a chance!"

Hard as it is to believe, I didn't know what "Fatso" meant. I thought he might have been talking about another kid, who had big ears!

Now this seemed to me to be a pretty good assessment of the situation, and showing off, I repeated this, in a slightly louder voice.

"Be careful," somebody murmured. "He might hear you!"

Since Big Ears wasn't very near, I felt safe in repeating this insight, and of course, my best friend, Richard Stockton, was standing right behind me when I said it. About the time the first tear dribbled down his dusty, sweaty face, I realized what I had done.

Richard and I didn't see each other for a few days, and then he called one afternoon and we ate cookies in the cave.

I would like to think that over the years I have suffered more than Richard Stockton by this stupid, unwitting betrayal. I've tried to track him down, but no luck. And after all, what would I say? Best to murmur a prayer and ask for forgiveness.

I did hear that he had a distinguished career at some Ivy League school as a Professor of Classics, certainly out of *my* league! I'll bet he lost weight, married well, and played a damn good game of golf, and maybe even tennis. . . .

Chapter 25
Teachers

If you have been fortunate enough to have dined with somebody from the PGHS Class of 1947, you will no doubt have noticed the impeccable table manners. I give credit for this social excellence to Mr. Val Clement, our Senior Problems teacher.

I suspect kids from Carmel and Monterey grew up knowing which fork to use, but in PG we seemed to be more interested in getting to the bottom of a root beer float with a straw. (Or maybe it was just me.) At any rate, Mr. Clement explained the nicety of holding the fork in the left hand, the knife in the right, cutting and eating one bite at a time. Never, never cut up the whole piece of meat before eating! And not only that, when finished eating, the knife goes on the plate, sharp edge *in*!

"Why?" said Mr. Clement. "To avoid cutting the servants!"

This was before we discovered pizza in our piney paradise, and the only servants we knew were in *Gone with the Wind*. I confess an occasional lapse these many years later, but try to remain correct when invited to lunch at Pebble Beach, the Country Club, or even Mission Ranch. And oh! One more thing. Never laugh at Easterners working on an artichoke for the first time! After all, how was your first exposure to soft-shell crab?

The other significant gem laid on us by Mr. Clement was How to Write a Check. High school seniors, 1947, had very little experience in this regard, but by golly, when we grew up and needed to pay a bill we sure knew where to put the dollars and cents, not to mention our signatures.

I know it's almost trite to say how much we owe our teachers, and not just what they taught us out of the book, but how they sometimes set us on the right path and all that. Trite but true. For stern but benevolent authority, how about our principal, A.B. Ingham? I seem to remember a tight little smile on his face as he roamed the halls. Once he noticed two boys trying to sneak a couple of ice cream bars into the library study hall. They'd stuck them in their pockets, and he said, "That's okay, boys. Just leave them there!"

As important as cutting your chicken-fried steak might be, it didn't come anywhere near preparation for the dreaded English A examination. Saving us from disaster was Miss Vega Swift, whom most of us remember as the best teacher we ever had. She rode a bike and hiked the John Muir Trail every summer, storing up enough patience to teach us how to diagram a sentence. As good as she was I could never grasp the concept, but managed to pass the test anyway. Possibly on good looks.

Teacher talk always triggers memories and comparisons, and I'll leave it to you to remember Miss Gardner, Mrs. Mello, Roger Matthews, Coach Baskin, and on and on. But with a nod to Monterey High, how about Miss Rendtorff? If conversation ever lags when talking to a Toreador, just mention her name. Gertie, they called her. She has been described to me as a sort of Mother Teresa with a whip! Dean of Women, she patrolled the halls preaching propriety, allowing no more intimacy than holding hands! A strict chaperone at school dances, she was also a very caring counselor if you needed one. I happen to live in the old Rendtorff home in Carmel, and I think she sometimes speaks to me in the dead of night.

Thank you, Lord, for all those who taught us. Look how well we turned out!

Chapter 26
Pull!

"PULL!" I'd shout, and my brother Brooks would sail a well-worn Decca out over the sand by Asilomar Beach while I blazed away with my 12 gauge shotgun. Hard to believe that during World War II shotgun shells were easy to come by, but there was a serious shortage of clay pigeons. Seems the Air Corps used them to train gunners. Equally hard to believe, but it was okay to fire shotguns on Asilomar Beach. Just try that today!

As luck would have it, we had lots of old phonograph records, and it seemed very patriotic to hone our shooting skills. I hate to think now what musical treasures we might have destroyed, but the good news is that the records didn't shatter as anticipated. Matter of fact, they didn't seem break at all. (I'm *sure* I hit them.)

After five or six pulls we moved on to other sport. There may be a broken record or two in the sand, these sixty years later, so watch your step.

All this comes to mind after reading about the Dick Cheney quail shoot in Texas. A couple of words about my shotgun. Dad got it through some surplus sale, a well-worn 12 gauge that had been shortened and used as a riot gun, or whatever. It was extended to legal length by a Cutts Compensator, a fixture to alter the pattern of shot, or some such. Unfortunately, it had the habit of going off, firing without provocation or a moment's notice. This made guys I hunted with very nervous and I was forced to hunt by myself. BANG. A gunsmith noted that the sear—some sort of latch to prevent premature firing—had been filed down, presumably to also prevent riots. The last time I used it was on the bluff just across the road from Rancho Cañada. After school one afternoon I planned to bring home a limit of quail.

I flushed a covey—scared me almost to death—but aimed nevertheless and pulled the trigger. Instead of the expected BANG, there was a muffled cough, and the shot, the BBs, rolled down the barrel into the grass at my feet. No quail, but Mom had a couple of chickens anyway, just in case. I haven't aimed in the general direction of quail ever since.

The 12 gauge stayed in the gun rack for a long time. A few seasons later it almost blew off brother Tom's foot—just missed— and he threw it in the river.

Chapter 27
Little Grains of Sand

Memory is a flawed reference, at best, but fortunately we can enhance our recollections with a happy tweak or a melding of adventures long ago. Dates and years in which such and so happened are especially tough, but no matter. When I came home from college, the pines up Carmel Hill had been replaced with a freeway. The other day I wandered into the Pacific Grove Library, still an absolute gem, and looked for the kids' section where I had spent much of my life. Gone, of course; moved and enlarged. I asked about the old Captain Cook South Seas collection, held under lock and key in the old days. The nice librarian had never heard of it.

What *did* we call the sand dunes? Asilomar Dunes? No, those were different. Del Monte Dunes? No, no. Well, no matter. When we said "Let's go out to the sand dunes," we knew what we meant.

Those dunes, now long gone, were magnificent treasures and should have been preserved as a national monument. They were huge, almost glistening white with a few pines in between. As kids we ran up and down, hid and hollered, rolled and slid, and then walked home along the railroad track. During the war we played soldier, heaving pinecones as grenades. We were spies, or scouts, sneaking up to peek on lovers doing strange things, things we might have done later ourselves.

At the edge of the dunes, the Sand Plant steadily munched

away our beautiful playground—with mechanical shovels and conveyer belts, yard by yard—then shipped it away, hopper by hopper, bag by bag, grain by grain. We told ourselves that our sand was so pure it was used to make bombsights or binoculars. Somebody said Coke bottles, but we didn't believe them.

Ah, the stories we could tell. Like the night a half dozen guys from the PG Rec Club heard that some Carmel types were having a bonfire, and who knows, maybe a beer out in the dunes. School spirit ran high in those days, and these Breakers planned to sneak up a dune, then charge down on those Padres and have a fun fight, or whatever. Sure enough, they peeked over the dune and there they were, a scant hundred yards away. Screaming like banshees with wild obscenities, they charged full-tilt down the dune, discovering, too late, that the Sand Company had stretched barbed wire in that particular location. They all hit the wire at the same time, and the tone of their screams intensified, with even more obscenities. The Carmelites hardly seemed to notice and continued their weenie roast.

Back at the Rec Club there were tales of bloody conflict, but the Breakers admitted to themselves that they had been *had*.

Even as the sand dunes diminished, they were still a place of love, lust, and general indiscretion. Fights were fought, scores settled, promises made, promises broken. I think the ghosts of the old Bohemians (from Carmel, of course) lurked in the shadows and watched us drink beer, laugh, and cry—and gradually grow up. We learned a lot in those dunes, like never make serious love in the sand, be sure to bring a blanket, and even then. . .

After the sand and the Sand Plant were gone and all that was left was a ragged mess, we wondered why hadn't somebody *done* something to save the dunes? But then, of course, we moved away, found our mates, built our lives, went off to war, came home again. Out of the mud came Spanish Bay; not bad, we said. Looks pretty darned good. Not the same, but still pretty good; complete, we think, with an occasional indiscretion. A few of *our* old ghosts still roaming around?

No, no. That's the bagpiper!

Chapter 28
Music

"The Bells of Hell may ting-a-ling for you, but not for me!"

This profound message appears under a work of art in the men's room at the Bay Wolf Café in Oakland. The meaning is somewhat elusive, but I find it nevertheless appropriate.

My struggle with music has been lifelong and never-ending. *Appreciation* is not the problem. That's always easy to fake—just smile and nod your head, maybe tap your foot, and nobody knows. I really do like most things; have a little trouble with Aaron Copland—heresy!— and off-key sopranos, but aren't most of them?

Just give me Jimmy Buffett and Willie Nelson almost any time, but my point of suffering really isn't *appreciation*. It's *performing*!

It's easy enough to sing bass, which is very forgiving, loudly, loudly in unison. Take "God Bless America," for instance. But what I really wanted to do, all my life, was play the piano. Truth is I didn't want it bad enough to really practice. It was more fun to sit down at the piano and bang out "She Reminds Me of You," now my entire rep, or "Sentimental Journey," now long forgotten.

When I was roughly nine or ten I had my first violin lesson. Aunt Molly, who lived in Lost Hills, of all places, had a fiddle left over from her husband, long gone, and a couple of thick cymbals. Cymbals still around, never played, but the violin seemed like too good a thing to pass up. This was, by the way, when kids were being solicited to play the accordion, buying one with lessons thrown in. Accordion bands, trips to Washington, DC, and so on, but the violin price was right, and off I want to Horace Mann Grammar School where Mr. Dayton taught everybody, regardless of instrument. As I walked in with my black violin case in hand, he was teaching some girl the fine points of the saxophone. He looked at me and said, "I'll be just a minute. Go ahead and rosin your bow."

Rosin my bow? What could he mean! I opened the case, took out the bow, looked at it, tightened and loosed whatever it was from top to bottom, not a *clue* about rosin. Finally the saxophone lesson concluded, and he got the picture. He gently pointed out the parts of the thing—bow, bridge, neck—and there in the bottom of the case was some rosin! That was enough for the first day, and the good news is that the next weekend I fell out of a rope swing in Kernville, shattered my elbow, and couldn't even play an accordion!

My mom was an accomplished pianist and organist, but those genes didn't trickle down to me. Mike got enough to sit down at the keyboard, and could even sing and dance. Tom was very good on the saxophone and even played in the Stanford band. Hit a protester of some sort on the ten-yard line with his sax and saved the day for US of A! Brooks was competent with the baritone horn, and Shirley, naturally, was and is dynamite on the piano. Once upon a time we all played at once—the parlor was called the Music Room—performing our favorite Christmas carol, all at the same time. A sort of contrapuntal exercise, not unlike a round—you know, like "Row Row Row Your Boat"—and just right for high hilarity and the holiday spirit. Dad was especially impressed, and even teared up a little. Had to go to the bathroom for "Kleenex" (i.e., bottle of vodka outside the bathroom window). Dad often tried to play the piano using the "Think" method, à la *Music Man*, but somehow he just didn't think enough.

Mom told me for years that if I worked hard enough on the piano I would be a social success when and if I went away to college. As it turned out, I guess, I worked just hard enough, because, by golly, I *was* a social success. Had nothing to do with the piano, and I successed myself right out of college after two years. (Back later, with *honors*, but that's another story.)

The big deal in high school was to be part of a band, and not just the PG High School Marching Band, where I happily played the bass drum, but a band that admiring friends danced to.

To satisfy this need for recognition, a few of my pals—all musically talented except me—formed a group, with me to play the piano. I think this was due to my organizational talents and the fact that my mother was the only mom that would let us practice in her house. Best musician in the crowd was George Mattos, who went to fame and fortune with the clarinet. (On another note, he also went to the Olympics twice as a pole vaulter.)

At any rate, I couldn't read music fast enough to keep up with the rest of the guys, and I was always three measures late at the end of the piece. Still playing, as it were, while the rest went out for a Coke. After a while, they suggested that maybe if I *started* two or three measures early—that is, before they did—we might all end up at the same time! It worked, but sadly, it sounded like hell, and I was transferred to the drums, where at least I wouldn't play off-key. Johnny Price took over on the piano, and he, as you know, was terrific. Didn't even have to read music!

The possible apex of my piano career came over Monterey radio station KDON in my senior year. One of our high school teachers had devised a radio script with some social message and enlisted half a dozen of us to read this thing on the air. He instructed us that radio commentators simply dropped their scripts after reading rather than shuffle papers noisily in front of the microphones.

There we were, nervous and shaking, rushing through fifteen minutes of script in five minutes, throwing paper to the winds. We stood there in great relief, but heavens! Ten more minutes to fill!

"Well," said the teacher, "Phil, how about a number on the piano?"

And by golly, there was a piano right there! Now keep in mind, the entire radio audience of the Monterey Peninsula was listening. What to do, except comply?

I wiggled my fingers and ripped through "She Reminds Me of You."

"Wonderful," said the teacher. "How about another one?"

Sure enough, I waddled through "Sentimental Journey," grateful for all those years of lessons.

"Swell," said the teacher. "We have five more minutes."

After another "She Reminds Me of You," and yet another "Sentimental Journey," the day was done, the Bells of Hell having ting-a-linged for me.

Once I was off to college, I achieved some success as the Phi Delt Chorister, singing songs in unison to uncritical sorority girls.

Not leaving well enough alone, Jim Woodman and I formed a duo called the College Cut Ups. Why, I'll never know, but we *could* have become contenders. Jim was especially strong on the ukulele, and I, never having seen one, decided to make and play a gutbucket. Mine was made of a washtub, two by fours with a hinge and a broken gut from the Music Department, tied and strung. Heavy and clumsy, but it worked. We played and sang old favorites, like "Five Foot Two" and "If You Knew Susie"; we told jokes and made happy fools of ourselves. Those were pioneer days in TV, and the local station, trying to fill time, booked us one afternoon. We went through our routine, having the nonexistent audience sing along, following a bouncing ball which went flat after the third bounce, but no matter. Great critical acclaim, and we were booked at the Saturday Matinee at the Kimo Theater, a great kids' show, between movies, with kids and moms filling the place.

For some dumb reason the curtain opened with us and our gear covered with white sheets. An alarm clock went off and we jumped out of the sheets, dressed in long johns, playing and singing "Ain't She Sweet." The kids were somewhat puzzled, but what the hell, this was Albuquerque, 1950! A smattering of applause, mostly their mothers, as we cavorted around the stage. Then, one of those odd moments, in between cheers, when the theater was silent, and some smart-assed kid in the front row stood up, pointed at Woodman, and shouted, "Mister, your balls are showing." And indeed they were. Well, what to expect, borrowed long johns and all.

Jim lowered his uke, went into a fast reprise, and we scooted offstage and out into the afternoon. Two or three more gigs, and then when invited to play at the Menaul School for the Feeble Minded—seriously—we decided to retire while on top and spend more time on our studies. Or something else, as it were.

The apple falls close, as they say, and my kids and grandkids will be at the top of the charts, just you wait and see. Scott and his buddies were famous in the East Bay in the '70s as the T Birds, a rock 'n' roll type doing things like "Teen Angel" and "Chantilly Lace." If you know the right Web site, you can still see them. Laura achieved a certain amount of fame with her piercing whistle, and Carrie does a great Patsy Cline. John and Matthew are actors, Greg and Andy *very* good on the guitar, both playing and writing music. Kelly and Melissa do hot piano and have also been known to sing.

Now I think I'll go downstairs and brush up on "She Reminds Me of You"—just in case. And by the way, I was pretty good on "Smoke Gets in Your Eyes," too.

II. COMMENTARY

Chapter 29
Cottage Requiem

In Carmel we treasure our old cottages and tend to happily remember the early occupants who were pulled to this part of the world by the things we still enjoy today—trees, ocean, an almost perfect climate, and a little quirkiness in our attitudes. There are the usual attempts to save the structures built by professors, artists, bohemians, and poets, but one by one, like Green Gates, they splinter away.

We all have life expectancies, and so do most of the cottages in Carmel. Green Gates across the street from me actually lived a few years beyond. Her soul went out with her lights when Willie (short for Wilhelmina) died two or three years ago.

Willie had lived in Green Gates for thirty-five years, not long by Carmel cottage standards, but long enough. She took great care of the place, raking, gardening, and repairing, making a home for herself and several generations of cats. Until yesterday the old Siamese still slept through the warm days on the shingle roof.

This was not a place where poets met and sang the abalone song, but there was a tryst or two back in the early days, or so we hear and like to believe. Teachers and librarians rented, then came and went, and during the war a colonel with his wife and daughter called it home. After he was killed on Guadalcanal they moved away, back to Santa Barbara where she remarried after the war. A few years ago I met her, standing by Green Gates, looking and remembering. She said they had been happy there. Her daughter was now a teacher, married, and living in Denmark, of all places. She took a picture, then left.

Not too many years ago a couple of aging hippies rented Green Gates North, a little cottage right behind Willie's. Their main intent, I surmised, was garage sales—small ones, since there just wasn't much surplus stuff from either Green Gates to be sold. Nobody stopped to look or buy, but the senior hippies, smiling, appeared to enjoy sitting in the sun anyway. The cottage was a lovely backdrop.

It seemed just right that Willie took up residence in Green Gates when she retired. She and the cottage were perfect caretakers of each other. While she was able, Willie walked up into town a couple of blocks away to pick up her mail and groceries. During baseball season you could see her TV screen, blinking away without a sound. She was deaf as a post, but that didn't keep her from smiling and saying hello.

Green Gates consisted of a single story with a garage for herself and one for Green Gates North, just behind, on the same double lot. It was a nice Carmel gray with green trim, and had a lattice fence and a gate with a faded sunflower. She was probably built by Michael Murphy, who had done half the village and had no grand pretensions of Julia Morgan or the Greene brothers. But there she was, "old Carmel," with a shrinking glimpse of the bay. People stopped to admire her, wishing she were theirs. Then, once Willie was gone, she was on borrowed time. The place seemed to sag, home only to a clutch of raccoons and maybe a rat or two.

The site is almost sacred, and it was inevitable that Green Gates would not be allowed, like old soldiers, to just fade away. Another few years and she would have just crumbled, but yesterday, along came the huge excavator—the cottage mortician, so to speak. The scruffy tea trees were axed, the lattice fence collapsed, and then, with almost a gentle reverence, the giant shovel invaded the kitchen roof, and away she went. When the brick chimney tumbled into the sun porch, it was clear that any remnant of her soul had left. A sad departure? Sure, but how much better to crunch and haul away then to let her just crumble in ancient disrepair.

1I'll miss looking out at Green Gates. I'll miss that pleasant wave of Willie's when she raked the leaves, and I'll miss the old Siamese.

Green Gates was an important part of my address: "On Camino Real, across from Green Gates!"

"Oh yes," they'd say. "We know the place!"

In a few months I'll be able to say, "across from that beautiful new house."

Adios, Green Gates! You were a great neighbor.

Chapter 30
Hieroglyphics

"On a day like today, we whiled our time away, writing love letters in the sand": Nothing quite captures the soupy sentimentality of transitory romance like that lyric. Pat Boone almost wrecked it, but sweet Patsy Cline lifted it up to a minor classic. This seemed to sum things up as we drifted in and out of love in the '30s, '40s, and even the '50s.

Those who were more certain of undying devotion, however, would find wet cement in freshly poured sidewalks. Luckily for us, these hieroglyphics remain underfoot to this very day.

These permanent palettes attracted more than just Valentines; as you wander around San Francisco, for instance, you will find some very interesting messages and works of art. Where Columbus and Montgomery meet, there is the wonderfully cryptic message MR. WONG GOES TO LUNCH. Local research sheds no light on the subject.

But back to our local lore. Carmel is a little sparse, with new sidewalks of brick and exposed aggregate, but the sandstone rocks on the beach, laid bare by winter storms, are richly inscribed with all sorts of sentiment. We can only hope that the elements will eventually wipe these slates clean.

Of a more permanent nature is the lovely sentiment at the southwest corner of Ocean and Casanova: STEVE + PAM, **1989**. Simple on the surface, but did Pam love Steve, too? Or did Pam inscribe this herself to make Sally jealous? Are they still an item? Did love last? And where are they now?

Across from Church of the Wayfarer, somebody spelled out VENDETTA, which could be scary—or maybe not. And we note across from L'Escargot that DICK LOVES (loved?) MARTHA.

Pacific Grove and Monterey inspired more rapture, requiring concrete proof and commitment. The early sidewalk contractor, W.H. Ten Eyck, signed his work and left room for romance, but I suspect those so noted moved on and left their marks elsewhere as well. There's a nice heart without other comment in front of the the Red House, and we note that ML did indeed love SH—or at least so it says behind Holman's. On that hallowed corner, 18th and Laurel, we see that CLUB YELLOW met and scattered about the names of a few members, including NEAL, JOHN, and most notably, LUNCHBOX KATE. Just across the street, CHUCK and FATIMA are set in concrete, so it says.

In Monterey on Pacific, ANTHONY AND ANGIE are forever together, and not far away there's a fine display of crosses and a bunch of roses, all in black and white. Doubtless the work of Serra's boys.

In those days most of us carried pocketknives, and as passion followed us through the woods we sometimes noted on an available oak that GP + PK, or DG + JD. And all this brings us back to "Love Letters in the Sand."

And the current trend to tattoos? That's altogether another story,

WHEN THE LORD SPOKE

Chapter 31
Home, Sweet Home!

Here we are, back from the pleasures of travel in Europe. No slides, but I know you're anxious to hear all about it. Delightful, beautiful, historic, and foreign, but let me tell you, if you ever think Ocean Avenue, Cannery Row, or the Concours Races and AT&T rolled into one are crowded, try Cinque Terra and Venice *after* the high season! Compared to those throngs, all speaking in tongues, Mission Ranch on Saturday night seems positively lonely.

What a relief was beautiful Slovenia! Green, quiet, wonderful people, wine and food, and spectacular Alps! We were spoiled early by a week's stay in the Savoie district of France, near Albertville, Chambery, and it if weren't for Carmel I think I could live there. Enough English understood for survival, and "*Van Blonk, por favor*" usually did the trick.

I'm told that I should have seen Venice thirty years ago, like other things in life. And yes, I did get lost three or four times (two nights, one day). If Venice sinks—predicted—it's because of the weight of the tourists. More people than pigeons, all with cameras and cell phones. Good food, good wine, and charming locals when you could find one. And ah, the romantic gondolas. I wasn't sure what to expect, but they reminded me of the evacuation from Dunkirk. Whole families, wide-eyed and happy, looking up at us looking down. Keep in mind that all the traffic in Venice proper is by boat—gondolas, water taxis, police, ambulances, garbage, and freight. When the tide comes in, you can borrow boots.

This isn't meant to be a travelogue, but I must add that our best meal was in Geneva, with great food everywhere else. I did have a bad mushroom in Bologna and lake fish with too many bones in Bellagio, but otherwise the cheeses, pastas, sausages, and greens, not to mention the wines one more time, were perfect.

And this time I really mean it. I'll never again fly more than two hours without First Class or Business seating! Matter of fact, I may never fly again, *period*! After all, you can drive to Big Sur in less than an hour, eat at Nepenthe, and be home before dark. Carmel Valley wines are as good as you can get, and you can push your luck and hit Soledad or Paso Robles. Our Farmers' Markets rival those of Bologna, and if you insist on hearing people speak Italian, it's only a couple of hours to North Beach.

As the old ads said, "See America First." Maybe too late for that, but how about *now,* starting with Monterey County? Ever been to the Pinnacles?

Chapter 32
Second Oldest Profession

I am living proof that the easiest person to sell something to is another salesman, current or past. In the last month I have bought magazine subscriptions, Omaha steaks, frozen shrimp, marinated tri-tips, somebody's cookies, and contributed to several charities, all at my front door. This goes back almost seventy years when I was the kid ringing doorbells. For those of you who also stood on the welcome mats, you understand that once initiated you are forever a member of the sales fraternity. You *understand* the brave but sometimes plaintive approach: "You wouldn't like to buy some Christmas seals, would you?" The kid has just knocked on the door, almost praying that nobody was home.

You remember that proud, exciting moment when you first slung the canvas bag over your shoulder, the one emblazoned with "*Liberty* magazine," and then off to the neighborhood, filled with hope and confidence. There weren't too many spare nickels around in the late 1930s, but there was always some kind soul who made other rejections all worthwhile. And moving on from *Ladies Home Companion* and *Country Gentleman*, it was vegetable and flower seeds, soap, salve, and greeting cards.

This experience suited me well as I moved on in college to ladies' shoes. Even though everybody is born barefoot, the need to acquire a nice patent leather pump with ankle straps takes skilled persuasion.

On to stocks, bonds, and financial security for both me and the clients. Apple from the tree, my son sold drugs for Pfizer and now helps people "shift assets" as a stockbroker. My oldest daughter sold batteries for Union Carbide and is now a writer, and my youngest sells real estate, after a brief fling selling Cutco knives, and even more successfully, dry martinis. Yes, they buy a lot of things, too.

When I was eight or nine, in Bakersfield, a salesman was trying to sell my mother a vacuum cleaner. He pulled out all the stops—flour in the carpet, lint from the mattress, an attachment to kill moths. My mother really did want that vacuum, and this was his second visit. As he started his close, Mom said, "I'm sorry, but we just don't have the money." We really didn't. The guy packed up his vacuum and replied, "And my family won't have a turkey for Thanksgiving!"

"Boy," I thought. "What a tough way to make a living." I think I've been trying to help that man get a turkey ever since.

Aside from the peddlers who appear on my doorstep, there aren't as many real salespeople anymore. We seem to buy what we need at the big box stores; the Watkins man, the Fuller Brush man, the Avon lady, and the Liberty kids aren't knocking on our doors. But don't give up hope for the endangered sales professionals. There's always the guy with half a cord of split oak left over on his truck, the young man working his way through something or other, the cute kid with a box of cookies, and the evangelist selling salvation. Just for fun, stroll by the booths at a County Fair, and you might even buy a pot, pan, or knife sharpener. Don't even think about the Internet or, God forbid, the telemarketers!

As for me, friend, I'm over budget, but maybe that guy next door.

Chapter 33
Nice to See You

Name scramble is a very tough thing to handle, almost as bad as name blackout. I find I can fake my way through blackout—forgetting who in the hell I'm talking to—with a smile and the old "Good to see you" gambit. "How's it going?" "I know, I know, it must be tough." But when, full of confidence, you call Jim Jack or Susie Sally, it's a little more difficult to recover.

This occurred to me today in church when two or three pews ahead sat the Saunderses, and a pew ahead of them, the Sanderses. I've known both couples for years, and mumbled through greetings, but there's always the peril of having to introduce them to somebody new. To make it worse, Sanders's first name is John, and Saunders's is Jim. I think. Maybe Saunders is John and Sanders Jim, but you can see the problem. The good news, of course, is that both the ladies are named Anne—although I can't be too sure. Just the other day I saw Mrs. Sanders, or Saunders, and knew I was safe. Her name is the same as Saunders/Sanders, so I cheerily said "Good morning—" And I blanked.

"Well," I surged on. "How's old (Jim? John?) How's your dog?"

"Dead," she said. She waved and was off.

One of my former associates got around all this with the wide use of "Tiger!" or "Tige!" This failing or faltering, he would say "Old fighter!" Inane at best, stupid at worst.

My bailout is usually "Coach!," said as if you were surprised and pleased to see him.

"Captain" sometimes fits, unless—as I was once reminded—he happens to be a *Colonel.* Then, too, there's the old Gov'nor!, or Senator, but some don't take likely to the insult.

For the ladies we have the old standards Sweetheart! Bright Eyes! Darlin'! But these can easily lead to all sorts of trouble. If the name escapes just say "How *nice* to see you!"

Possible trouble there too, but better odds.

Pronunciation is crucial, unless you whisper, or cough into your Kleenex. Being very conscious of this issue, I always introduce myself as "Bowhay, rhymes with Maui!" Why, just the other day a lady in Safeway said to me, "I'm sorry I can't remember your name, but I know it sounds like Honolulu!"

Chapter 34
Ink

I'll bet the gang at the *Herald* would agree that printer's ink on your hands, face, and in your blood early enough never really rubs off. I haven't been in a press room lately, but boy, if I close my eyes and take a deep breath I can remember that wonderful smell of ink, newsprint, and molten lead. I can still hear the rumble of the press and the clatter of the linotype, and there I am, maybe twelve years old, sitting on the floor in the middle of all this, wrapping three hundred *Advertisers* to be delivered the next morning. All this at the *Tide*, Pacific Grove's finest weekly, under the direction of Bill Gould, on Forest, right across from City Hall. Bill had a small crew to handle the machinery, but he knew every nut, bolt, and gear on the press and could work the linotype, load the newsprint, and sweep the floor. He wrote with flair, handled the circulation, hustled the advertisements, and inspired the paperboys. After he sold the paper to a lesser god, Mr. Keppleman, Bill taught journalism at San Jose State. The paper changed from the *Tide* to the *Pacific Grove Tribune*, and while Kepp was a good journalist, he wasn't really part of the town. The big buzz was that he had worked for *Life* magazine!

On my rickety Schwinn I threw papers sooner or later at every house above Lighthouse. Up at 4:30, rain or shine, after a hot cup of Postum I hit the road. With the *Advertiser*, the *Tide*, and then the *Herald*, and on to the *Chronicle*, I spread the news. I might note that Pacific Grove is very chilly in those last hours of dark in the morning. Not much for the business side of journalism, I didn't enjoy "Good evening! Collecting for the *Herald*!" Too often I'd hear "Kid, come back tomorrow." Sure, sir. One more tomorrow and no *Herald*!

Although I wrote a misbegotten column or two for the *Tribune*—irresponsible and immature, at best—I got my Big Break when Reg Murphy graduated from PGHS and introduced me to Ted Durein, Sports Editor, at the *Herald*. For a glorious year I covered, with a *byline*, Pacific Grove High School games. Trite ("Jerry Fry played his usual heads-up game"), but I was *in print*, and not only that, I got a dime an inch!

Best of all, and this goes back to the printer's ink, were the early mornings in the *Herald* office, sitting at an old Smith Corona in the same room with Durein and Joe Costello, real newspapermen! I could smell the ink, the newsprint, the melting lead, the coffeepot, the creosote cough drops. I could listen to the banter, hear the teletype, and know that I was part of this marvelous world. Actually *in* the paper, moving up a notch from tossing it up on a porch!

Soon enough I was on to other things, where a dime an inch wouldn't pay the rent. In the meantime, when I hear "I really liked your column in the *Herald*," I wish I could hear Bill Gould say he really liked it, too.

Chapter 35
No Idle Hands in PG!

Strolling up and down Lighthouse, Alvarado, and Ocean Avenues we notice a lot of kids working and a lot who are not. That's okay, of course, since those not *obviously* working are probably computer experts who do things online for fun and profit. Things best we not know about, or even understand. Pushing a broom, sweeping sidewalks, clerking, and waiting at tables, we understand. Heck, we've done it!

Back in the good old days, the '40s, with World War II before and after, there was plenty of work around for the local kids, and no child labor laws to get in the way. We started collecting pinecones, used for kindling, and I think we got paid a dime for a gunnysack full. Huckleberries were a little more seasonal, and those got us a buck for a quart Mason jar. Believe me, that's a lot of huckleberries.

We moved up the labor ladder to lawns and yard work, and I can tell you that as far as I could discover, nobody in PG had a decent, sharp lawn mower. (There's a war on, you know.) But we chewed up the grass, hit the edges with 1915 vintage clippers, and earned enough in an afternoon to buy a war stamp or two.

Sooner or later most of us boys got off to a good start in journalism, delivering newspapers from sea to shinning sea. Only two reasons to get out of bed at 4:30 a.m.—either paper routes or fishing.

The biggest and best employers were the Forest Hill Hotel and Holman's, and sooner or later most of us swept the walks, washed the windows, stocked the shelves, carried the suitcases, bused the tables, washed the dishes, raked the yard, carried the trash, and learned the pleasure of good, honest work, as our parents reminded us.

If you were lucky, you could clean out boats for Sprague, or you could caddy at the finest nine-hole course in the state. If you couldn't caddy, you could look for golf balls, or you could even unload lumber for the yard by the depot. Good, honest work! And don't forget the soda fountains.

The grocery stores and drugstores on Lighthouse exposed us to either possible future local careers or an urge to continue our educations.

I think Bill Hellum, Charlie Higuerra, Ken Zug, Vince Bruno, and Clyde Dyke hired and trained more kids than the WPA. My golly, the *secrets* discovered in the back room of a drugstore—the thrill of watching Bill Hellum carve up a side of beef, and learning how to snap a folded paper bag open! And with practice you could learn how to imitate a trombone, just like Bill!

I remember the summer the City of Pacific Grove hired me to fill in wherever needed—sweeping streets, collecting trash, figuring costs of new curbs and gutters. One fine day I filled the city dump truck with trash from cans all over town. Happily driving the truck back to the corporation yard, I pulled into the yard and noticed that the truck bed was up. No trash! I had pulled the wrong lever, or pushed the wrong button, and dumped the collected mess up and down the streets of the Last Hometown! What to do?

Well, it was quitting time. I decided then and there that I had better get serious about an education. Haven't been in a dump truck since.

Chapter 36
Hello, Central!

It has been a long time since Alexander Graham Bell asked Mr. Watson to come see him, and even longer since two cans and a string. I'd like to say that some of the magic is gone with the introduction of the iPhone, but magic it is. Just imagine! Taking a picture of your ear, transmitting an image of your nose, all while talking to Aunt Sally in Duluth!

As magic as it may be, some adjustment is necessary to punch in a number on a cell, having grown up with a rotary—remember the *dial?*—and Bell forbid if you try wearing mittens, or even gloves! You may also have noticed that you can't make an anonymous call anymore. Just as well.

I look back with nostalgic reverie to those days of triple-digit phone numbers—"Hello, Central! Give me 632!" or "Just connect me with Roy Wright. I need a pound of nails." In the '40s we expanded to four digits. All this on party lines, the greatest gossip facilitator, yet to be improved on.

Depending on where you lived, the caller cranked the handle on the wall phone, alerting all on the line that somebody wanted to talk. All subscribers had an assigned number of rings. In Kernville at the Ranger Station ours was short-long-short, Andrew Brown General Store was three longs, and if you forgot the number, just crank one long and ask Gertrude to help you out. "Hang up, Sarah. My barn's on fire!" If you asked Gertrude to connect you to Long Distance, you could hear the click, click, click as the neighbors picked up.

Time marched on and we moved into the romantic world of Exchanges. The phone company felt that it was easier for us to remember a word, followed by five numbers, than all seven digits at once. And then, too, there are more choices with the alphabet. The most famous was the Penn Exchange, Pennsylvania 6-5000. (Must be said in a loud voice, PENNSYLVANIA SIX FIVE THOUSAND!) Try shouting that into your cell.

San Francisco Chinatown had its own exchange, the operators knowing five dialects and English. Almost sounds familiar, doesn't it, although after awhile you do get used to that colorful Mumbai accent when you call for technical assistance.

The San Francisco Financial District was *EXbrook* and *TUxedo*. "*EXbrook 2-7211,* Dean Witter!" In the East Bay I think it was *THornhill*.

The last phone books with the exchanges listed are now collector's items, but having read this you probably don't need one anyway.

In good old Pacific Grove it was *FRontier*. "*FRontier* 5-3319. Bowhay residence!" Most of us in Pacific Grove had some experience with a switchboard—PBX—memorialized by Lily Tomlin. (The operators looked like they had a buffalo horn impaled in their chests.)

What next after Apple Phone? I read about some technology that would enable you to simply *think* of a number or the soul with whom you would like to communicate, but what would that do to Ma Bell or the other pretenders?

And there is the rumor that continued cell phone use might cause brain damage. *Might?* Just look at them!

Chapter 37
Raccoons

And lo, it came to pass that the Carmelites of the Village by the Sea ventured not out at night or even some in light of day, for fear of bodily harm inflicted by dreaded beasts that lurked in bushes, drains, and trees. Much wailing and loud lamentation, but the beasts feared not for certain odd folk still fed and nurtured them. Even those who toured from far counties, even those who cared not for extra tax at the inns, stayed home, fearing harm to those they begat. Then, lo and behold, those of Mitchell, Coldwell Banker, Pinel, and others said perhaps value of land and houses, yea, even in the Golden Triangle, might suffer, or even plummet through fear of beasty infestation. For reasons still not known, that did the trick, and within one month, yea even three weeks, the little bastards disappeared, some say by the hand of the City Council, or even the hand of God, but not even a carcass was to be found! May they rest in peace!

Chapter 38
Dogs

We all know that walking your dog on the beach is a sure way to meet people. This is especially true on Carmel Beach. Every day, it's "Nice dog!," "What a sweet pup!," "How old...," etc.

Why, just the other day a lady came down the sand with a beautiful, well-behaved chow, a breed I don't particularly like, but just to be polite, I said something like "What a beauty!"

The owner smiled, tugged at the leash, and said, "I love my dog. I've given up on men!"

Now that is a real showstopper response. If I had been lonesome, like some people I know, I could have said any number of things. After all, she was nice-looking, just a little overweight, but not bad, overall. I could have said, "Given up on men? You haven't tried me!" Or "Well! How about a cup of coffee?" Or "Some men *are* dogs! Take me, for instance."

Instead, I wisely said, "Heel, Molly, Heel! Good dog!" and walked on up the sand and into the car.

Chapter 39
Thanks, to Grandparents

Since my grandchildren are perfect—well, above average—I offer the following for other grandparents who have expressed dismay at a seeming lack of gratitude. You know what I mean. You happily send off to Mary or Roger a nice little check or a crisp piece of currency, along with a Merry Christmas or a Happy Birthday, signed "Love, Grandma or Grandpa." Right off the bat you know you don't really need a thank-you, but as the weeks go by you begin to wonder if the roommate went through the mail, or the post office screwed up, or whatever.

Let's be fair. These kids are busy. You know they opened the envelope with a smile and thought happily of you, and then rushed off to spend the loot—on what, I dare not think. But look at the diversions today! There are those video games that keep them up with technology; there is e-mail, YouTube, MySpace, and even homework! You wouldn't want *that* shorted, tuition being what it is today.

Still, you would like to know. So here's my plan. Start with the old S.A.S.E.: enclose with the etching of the President a self-addressed stamped envelope. This will be much appreciated, stamps costing as much as they do. That in itself might be enough, but to the heart of it all: I think a form to be checked might do the trick.

"THANKS, [grandma, grandpa], for the $$$! IT WAS MORE [or less] THAN I EXPECTED! I WILL SPEND IT [on books, beer, haircut, pizza, video game].

"THANKS AGAIN! LOVE _____."

There's always the possibility that this paperwork might fall off the desk, and along about next birthday or Christmas, you might send a card, with "Dear Mary (or Roger), This year I am sending your usual gift to the Salvation Army, in your name. I know this will please you. No need for you to acknowledge this. Love, Grandpa/Grandma."

Then be sure you do send that five bucks off to the Salvation Army! No cheating!

Chapter 40
Gilding the Lily

If you have lately visited Jackson, over in the Gold Country of California, you may have noticed that very few people are frowning. Maybe not smiling, either, but the point of this is that my brother Tom, a real country doctor, has changed the face of Jackson. Yes, indeed, in addition to treating most known maladies common to Amador County, Dr. Bowhay is the local Botox King!

You know, of course, that Botox erases frowns, enhances lips, lifts lids, and all manner of things to do with faces imperfect, or so imagined. This miracle drug, however, can help solve other problems, like sore joints, painful backs, and muscles acting out of sync. Early on Tom tried some of this on himself, just to make sure.

Family members and friends also sampled test injections—not me, Lord, not me!—and the rest, as they say in Jackson, is history. (I witnessed one of these injections on a sibling's wrinkled forehead and almost fainted.)

You may have read that a good slug of Botox does the trick for about three months, and then a tune-up is required. Naturally this is good business for Dr. Tom, but he is actually most interested in service to the human race.

At any rate, come Monday morning the ladies—mostly ladies—line up in the waiting room to get their three-month lip enhancement. Tom, of course, careful about overmedicating, insists that they be able to whistle before they get another shot.

Apparently there is a little "sting" as the juice is injected, and one lady claimed it hurt so much (very little tolerance) that after the left side of the lip was done she said "No more, no more!" A week later, with the left lip full and voluptuous and the right lip still plain old Sally, she came back, bit the bullet, and Tom finished the job.

Needless to say there are some stories that will amuse, but to Tom this really is serious stuff. You and I may believe that we have the face that we deserve, but this self-acceptance is not universal. *In most cases, Botox properly applied, enhances or restores self-esteem!* It doesn't take too much of a practiced eye to spot a little facial tune-up, and with it we notice a spring in the step, an assurance in the eyes, and a comparison to a "baby's bottom." No whistle, but you can hear them humming a happy little tune. Just look around some night at Mission Ranch in Carmel, or even in church on Sunday.

A long time ago when I was in a stockbroker training program, we were introduced to the art of Psycho-Cybernetics by Dr. Maxwell Maltz. I'm still not sure what all that had to do with selling securities, but it was fascinating just the same. Dr. Maltz claimed that plastic surgery, or a reconstructed face, dramatically improved the way patients saw themselves, *whether or not the job was well done!* This was way before Botox, and there may have been some apocryphal hyperbole in his claim. But let me tell you this. If you spend a few thou on your kisser, you're damned sure you look good!

On this whole body enhancement subject, you may remember the Carol Doda days in San Francisco. There were some engineering problems that I understand have long since been corrected. Once again, stroll through Mission Ranch some night and look around. And then, of course, the stories about too many face-lifts, such as the lady who had so many that every time she crossed her legs, she smiled!

Which leads to that great quote from a San Francisco doctor who said, "When will women learn it's not *how* they're built that counts, it's how they're *wired!*"

Chapter 41
Mal de Mer

Seasick! Why is it if you're not, and somebody else is, it's a little bit funny. Not really funny, but all pretense stripped away, self-respect be damned, and the victim too sick to ask for help or mercy. Usually, too, an epidemic with more than one afflicted, especially on a party boat. The term "party" seems out of place at times like that, but there it is, and not even a shred of camaraderie. Those who are able crawl into the cabin and lie there in silent misery. Those who can't crawl roll around in the scuppers, hoping to die.

My mother couldn't even walk out on the wharf without getting queasy, and brother Brooks, a deep-water sailor in fact, inherited this tendency. As kids our fishing routine included a pancake breakfast, then rowing a skiff out from the wharf. Brooks was the only person I knew who could throw up and smile at the same time.

A true sufferer needs no trigger, but there are usually some fine fellows who start the morning with red wine or beer and a rotten cigar. Throw in some diesel fumes, some gentle swells, and that's all she wrote.

There's lots of lore on prevention and cure, and the patch behind the ear really does seem to do the trick, especially if applied before exposure, so to speak. Old story, probably out of *Reader's Digest*: Lady asks Captain, "What will I do if I get seasick?" Captain answers, "Don't worry, lady. You'll do it!"

A long time ago my dad, who never got seasick, or poison oak, for that matter, went out fishing with his four-year-old grandson Mike

(Brooks's son). The poor kid was very miserable sick. My dad said, "Mike, eat this sandwich and I promise you'll never get seasick again. Okay?"

Out of the lunch bucket, rye bread, Monterey sardines, and a big slice of red onion, down the hatch, and Mike swears he has never been seasick since!

The other surefire cure is two hours under an oak tree.

Chapter 42
Hark, How the Bells!

Christmas was made for Pacific Grove, or maybe it was the other way around.

The New England traditions were in full bloom, wreaths and holly (from the Holman ranch near Watsonville) and trees trimmed with those old-fashioned ornaments and strings of lights that didn't work. What a thrill to open the ornament box and find last year's strings of popcorn and wads of tinsel! As kids we *knew* that the North Pole wasn't some place above Canada. The North Pole was *Holman's*! The place just *smelled* like Christmas, with Santa sitting up on the mezzanine surrounded by kids and toys and anxious parents. In the back, next to the stairs, moms were busy redeeming fat books of S&H Green Stamps. Out in front on Lighthouse, the Salvation Army Band promised "Joy to the World," and one lucky December they let *me* play the bass drum. Real trees were tied to the lampposts—no aluminum fakes in *our* town.

If Mrs. Sees was around then, she was outdone by Whitman's Sampler, sold by the dozens from Dyke's Grove Pharmacy—the corner of Forest and Lighthouse, still the center of town. Warren Claunch, with a red scarf around his neck, sold copies of the *Herald* and graciously received year-end tips. Right across the street the windows of Varian's Barber Shop were smeared with soapsuds snow, and bunches of mistletoe hung round about. A kiss here and there on rosy cheeks, with runny noses wiped on sleeves. It was a season to be jolly!

Late in the day carols chimed from the City Hall Clock Tower, and on an occasion or two I was allowed to play them on the little keyboard, now sitting in the corner of the Heritage Barn. (The *keyboard* is in the barn, not me.) The chimes in the tower—and the clocks—were given to Pacific Grove by my grandmother in honor of her husband, Sumner E. Philbrick. (That explains how I got my name—Philbrick. And here all along you thought it was a misprint! That's why I use Phil.)

Possibly the biggest deal in town was the Singing Christmas Tree. This was a tree-shaped platform, maybe fifteen feet high, built on a vacant lot on Pine, with about thirty members of the Pentecostal Church perched on different levels, singing carols loud and clear. (Beat *that*, Garrison Keillor!) And did every church in town stage a pageant, or just Mayflower Congregational? At any rate, the Virgin Mary got more beautiful every year. Just remember, our mothers reminded us, Christmas is Jesus's Birthday. Happy Birthday, Jesus, and Merry Christmas!

Our high school glee club also sang, pure as gold, and I still remember the shiver when Barbara Williams hit that solo high note in "O Holy Night."

PG was still dry, except for a drop or two in the hard sauce that went with everybody's persimmon pudding. But if the town was dry, why indeed did our house, on Christmas Day, smell faintly of bourbon? "Not me!" said Dad.

The scurry of Christmas morning—cologne for Mom, Camels for Dad—and around town saw kids pedaling new bikes, skating on new skates, and tossing new balls; everyone was happy in varying degrees. Dinner was always great, with plates around town to the old and the shut-ins. And then, relief. Christmas was over.

You may think that all stockbrokers are rich, but I remember a Christmas a long time ago when my wife and I were *broke*. Happy, but broke. Couldn't afford a tree from the Scout lot, so we chopped down a five-foot holly in the backyard. It was a pretty little thing, but dangerous to decorate, and after a week or so, it dried out completely. Our kids that year got homemade fiberboard bulletin boards, and my wife and I exchanged kisses. (Beat *that*, O. Henry!)

Merry Christmas, etc., etc. When you walk by Holman's, give it a wave. Santa will see you.

WHEN THE LORD SPOKE

Chapter 43
Christmas in PG

And lo, it came to pass, Christmas again in Pacific Grove! Christmas everyplace else, I know, but we had Holman's, and more to the point, we had us! The 1940s were both sweet and sad with the war full-blown, friends and relatives overseas, soldiers and sailors here, ready to go. The radio played "I'll be home for Christmas, you can count on me," but not quite, in 1942 or 1943. We prayed in church, sang our carols, and hoped for heavenly peace, but even with solemn overtones, Pacific Grove was joyful, happy, and enthusiastic with the Christmas spirit.

Santa was on the mezzanine in Holman's, right in front of the electric train spectacular. Little kids, all bundled up, climbed on his lap; not realizing that it is more blessed to give than receive, they asked for the moon. In return for their innocent faith, they got a candy cane from the elf alongside. You could hear "Silent Night" over the whoosh of the pneumatic tubes. We slightly older kids had worshipped the Wish Book, the Sears catalog, hopefully marking and folding pages in case Santa was confused. For a real trip down memory lane, log on to the S.S. Adams catalog with joy buzzers, whoopee cushions, and disappearing ink. Great gifts!

It was a struggle finding something to give to moms and dads, brothers and sisters, and close, close friends. But look! Look, here we are! A breadboard from woodshop, or a towel holder with the sliding marble, or a photo taken at school, framed with green paper and cotton snow!

We treasure the story of Annie Guastella (with whom I was secretly in love, but then, who wasn't). She went to Rudy Partridge, president of the bank, and asked if she could borrow fifty dollars. He wanted to know why she needed it, and she said to buy Christmas presents for her parents and friends.

"Well," he said. "What is your collateral?" (She knew what that meant.)

"I'm your daughter Marie's best friend!" she said proudly.

"Good enough," said Rudy, and he wrote the check!

It seems to me that Christmas trees were a little hard to come by in the '40s (there's a war on, you know), but good old Del Monte Properties looked the other way as we lopped off a Monterey Pine and carried it home. It seemed just right. This all before Candy Cane Lane, but the town still glistened and glimmered, and no matter where you wandered you could hear people singing. When they weren't singing, you could hear the City Hall chimes intoning, "O Little Town of Bethlehem" and snug little town of PG!

Merry Christmas!

Chapter 44
Dress Right!

Back in the old days, between then and now, we used several stock market predictors, some more successful than others. The Super Bowl was one of the best—old NFL team wins, good market ahead. There was the Peruvian anchovy story—wheat blight someplace else in the world, some kind of Wave, sunspots, eclipses, not to mention buyers versus sellers. The best, of course, was the miniskirt theory. The shorter the miniskirt, or dress, the higher the market. I guess you could also say, "More leg, more money!"

To check this out, I wandered up to Ocean Avenue to make note. Friends, I hadn't realized how scarce a commodity skirts (mini or otherwise), dresses, or gowns have become. Ladies both young and not so young are putting on their pants, as the saying goes, one leg at a time. Jeans (both loose and tight), pants, slacks, trousers, pedal pushers, and clam diggers, all well and good, but darned few skirts. Oh, there are the tennis outfits, but since those were always short, they aren't much use in determining a trend. I did notice some short shorts, which deserve further observation. Then there is the tightness-of-jeans factor, which may be promising, but also dangerous.

This story is really more important for aesthetics than whether or not the market fluctuates in the right direction. Look back in your old yearbooks, magazines, and family photos, and appreciate the lovely look of dresses, short or long. The girls walked with a sort of swing and style that's impossible in blue jeans. Remember the word "flounce?" (The verb, not the noun.) "She flounced down the street, as delightful as a summer breeze, her dress swinging just above her knees." There was Marilyn Monroe, over the air jet, and high school dances where the girls spun and twirled, with lovely legs revealed. Girls even wore dresses to the Boardwalk, pretending they didn't know about the air jets in the Fun House!

It is still entertaining to study the styles on Ocean Avenue or Cannery Row and grudgingly appreciate those Calvin Kleins. A friend of mine who knows about such things claim that some strippers make an act of wriggling out their close-cut Levis. Then for an encore, they wriggle them back on!

So ladies, for the sake of your country, or at least the stock market, take that rebate check and buy a dress or skirt. Still discreet, but not too long.

I think I may have strayed from the subject, but in closing, "Never sell America short!" Or short short.

Chapter 45
The Hospital Parking Lot

I was in the parking lot of John Muir Hospital in Walnut Creek, anxious to get on the road to my home in Carmel before rush hour. My 50-year-old son had had back surgery, and it had been a long day. But the passenger side door on the car next to mine was open, and I had to wait while the lady inside looked in the rearview mirror, fiddled with her face, and dabbed her eyes. Seeing me, she apologized, stepped out, and closed the door. I could tell at a glance that she had been pretty once upon a time, but now looked like a case of too many cigarettes and barroom nights—skinny with longish blonde hair and a practiced, pleasant smile.

She told me she had brought her boyfriend in, that his heart had been pounding like crazy and she thought he might die. She went on to tell me that he was an alcoholic, too, and that she had given him a beer on the way over.

I fought the temptation to glance at my watch.

They both drank too much, she told me, and maybe this was a wakeup call. I told her she had done the right thing, bringing her boyfriend to the hospital, and that they were probably taking good care of him.

"You have a kid in there?" she asked, waving toward the hospital.

"Well, no," I said, then realized that I did, my 50-plus son with the back surgery. "But how about you?" I asked, moving things along.

"Yeah, my boyfriend. His heart's been pounding like crazy for three days and I finally got him to the emergency room. It was just pound-

pound-pound and I thought he might die." A touch matter-of-fact, but her eyes were crinkling, and she dabbed them with a tissue.

"You did the right thing," I said. "I bet he'll be okay."

"He's alcoholic, too."

"Oh, boy. How much does he drink?"

"About eighteen a day."

"Whatever it is, that's a lot! What does he drink?"

"Budweiser. He had one on the way over—we live in Antioch—and he said it made him feel better."

"That's an awful lot of beer. Rough on his liver, too."

"Yeah," she said. "I've got cirrhosis myself."

Oh, boy! Too many miles of bad road.

"Where you from?"

I said Carmel. She smiled, said you must know Clint.

"Sure," I said. "Now you take care. I think your boyfriend's going to be all right, but you be sure to get some help with your own liver. I'm going to pray for you both, but God can only go so far. You've got to meet Him halfway."

She smiled a thank-you, some tired charm still left from years ago.

I waved, and drove away.

Chapter 46
By God! By Golly

We don't hear it much anymore, but in the good old days we talked about "Monterey by the Smell," "Carmel by the Sea," and "Pacific Grove, by God!" Old-time Toreadors will remember that as a compliment, and let me hasten to reassure those from a later litter that the "smell" was a badge of distinction, no pun intended. Oh, sure. Gilroy, Hershey, Pennsylvania, and even Carmel Point at low tide have smells, but nothing like the Smell of Prosperity! Ours was a pungent reminder of the bounty of the bay, that the purse seiners had filled their nets, spilled the catch into the hoppers off the Row, and everybody had work! The smell, of course, didn't stop at the city line. It mixed with the plentiful PG fog; it settled and stayed in our hair, our clothes, and our very souls! Which brings me to PG by God.

You possibly didn't realize that God did indeed live in Pacific Grove. There are those who claim He still does, but a cruise through town suggests that maybe now just on weekends. When the magnificent Methodist-Episcopal Church (a cathedral, really) was demolished, the town lost a big hunk of its heritage. My Church Bell historian, Don Gasperson, and I well remember the Methodist Church Bell on Sunday mornings, and there must have been more, but memory fades. (Yes, I know. The Bells of Saint Mary's were Episcopal, too.) It should have been preserved as a National Monument, just like the sand dunes should have been, or at least allowed to burn. What a fire that would have made! But no, a wrecking ball, and away she went. If you didn't know, Chili Great Chili and other fine establishments took its place after years of an empty lot, forlorn and filled with trash. (I self-inflicted that awful movie, *A Summer Place*, just to show my friend that brief clip of the church—five seconds—and then back to Sandra Dee.)

But look at what we have left! Our ancestors built these sacred symbols with prayerful hands, hopeful hearts, and the certainty that Pacific Grove would always be a land of promise and holy refuge. I wandered into Mayflower the other day—formerly Mayflower Congregational, but Presbyterian is now close enough—and looked under the third pew on the right, thinking that my grandmother's footstool might still be there. Not, as they say.

In those hallowed days the minister ignored the subtle crackle of cellophane as grandmothers unwrapped peppermint drops for quiet kids. The church kitchen, like all church kitchens to this day, smelled faintly of natural gas. And those old churches all seemed to have wonderful cubbyholes, hidden rooms, nooks in the bell towers, and exciting places to hide. Mayflower is the only church I know that had a real live firing range in the basement, .22 shorts! We Boy Scouts in Troop 46 were ready for anything.

And now down Central to Saint Mary's Episcopal, an exact replica of a church in Bath, England. It's a religious experience just to step inside. Across the street, the Christian Church, straight out of New England, and further down, St. Angela's. Many more, just remember your own. We grew up with Sunday school and later youth groups and Christian rallies. Out of this reverent soup, several of our friends and colleagues heard the call and went into various levels of the ministry.

Evangelists loved Pacific Grove, with the highest conversion rate in the state. No matter how many times we were saved, another once or twice couldn't hurt. How could you *not* walk down the aisle!

In those holy years the town was dry, dry as a bone. The thirsty sinners could march up Forest, just across the line, and patronize Dode's, or slip into New Monterey—was it Cork and Bottle?—and then the Half Way House. When I suggested to my mother that Jesus had said something about a little wine being good for the stomach and that wine indeed was a miracle, she pointed out that wine in those days wasn't the same, and at any rate, He said "a *little* wine."

You may have noticed that things have changed in PG. Very few stomachaches!

Chapter 47
The Good Old Summertime

The good old summertime in Pacific Grove was just about as good as it gets. Fog in the morning when we did our chores and worked at our jobs, then between 11:00 and noon, out came the sun, and off we went to the beach, or up the valley to Schulte's swimming hole. Yep, there was water in the Carmel River!

We climbed on the rocks (Devil's Slide), baked in the sun, burned ourselves to blisters, and the girls lathered on baby oil laced with iodine. Good grief! But the tans were lovely and their hair sunstreaked with strands of blond. And oh my goodness, the legs!

Lucky as we were on our side of heaven, there was nothing to cap a trip to the Boardwalk, with thrills, chills, and super-excitement. There, indeed, were the most beautiful girls in the world, all at least two years older than me, and of course, they're still there today, about sixty years too young!

Remember how it all sounded? The clack, clack, clack of the Big Dipper as it climbed that first hill after coming out of the sudden dark? The pause at the top, screams starting, and then the thunderous roar, down and around, screams and hollers, hands in the air. That was, and is, the best roller coaster in the world. Solid and strong, and just the right rickety! Legend was that a Monterey kid, whose name I'd never tell, actually fell out of the Big Dipper, and not only lived, but went on to Cal, one of Pappy's Boys! You know how those stories go around.

We were never too old to ride the Merry-Go-Round, also the best in the world, and can't you still hear the music! Was it a calliope?

The Fun House, now long gone, had goofy mirrors, a super slide, a spinning disc, a rolling tunnel, and an air jet, like the one that caught Marilyn Monroe. "Oh, goodness!" said the girl from Carmel. "I had no idea!"

There were corn dogs, cotton candy, peanuts, popcorn and Cracker Jacks, Saltwater taffy to ruin your braces, and grease-dripping hamburgers that could ruin your ride home after a spin on the Tilt-o-Whirl. We tried our luck and skill at Ski Ball, darts at balloons, and baseballs at Hitler, Hirohito, and Mussolini. The Ricksen twins—Cal, NCAA, and all that—periodically wiped out the basketball concession. They'd finally quit when the guy ran out of stuffed bears. The Penny Arcade, also the best in the world, was filled with fun, with pennies to spend and sometimes nickels. The guys impressed gals with how much electricity they could hang on to, and then to the claw to grab a very valuable toy.

The Boardwalk sounded good and smelled good. It was a *real* magic kingdom, not like those pretenders of later years.

But back we always went to our own piece of heaven, with dances, picnics, card games, boat rides, beer busts, and walks around the Point and drops of fog in our hair. Sometimes a mild indiscretion or two, but no permanent harm done. Now, looking back, I think I'd like just one more ride on the Big Dipper. And no. No more indiscretions!

Chapter 48
Skin Deep...or Class Reunion Time Again!

Somebody once said that "Beauty is only skin deep, but ugly goes clean to the bone."

Now look back on it. When did you first realize that you were ugly? As in, clean to the bone. Kindergarten? First grade? Sooner or later somebody told you you looked funny. Maybe not quite ugly, but certainly not as good-looking as that other kid everybody seemed to like. Whether or not any of that was true is not the point. It stuck.

I remember asking my mom if I looked funny, and of course she told me I was very handsome. Getting right down to it I don't think it made a lot of difference in the long run (meaning seventy years later). For a long time, though, there was that persistent little doubt, with furtive glances at the bathroom mirror. Then there was the acne thing, which ruined any self-esteem I might have salvaged.

In the seventh grade at Pacific Grove Grammar School, I thought how much better off I'd be if I looked like Dick Baxter. Then in the eighth grade I thought maybe I'd rather look like Marty Larkin. By the time I got to high school I knew I was stuck with what I had and got used to it. A couple of years with the orthodontist helped, and I moved on from the green "stickum" that Mom used to plaster on my hair to Brylcream. "A little dab" didn't quite do it, but almost.

Girls, I thought, didn't seem to have this set of appearance problems. I mean, some were prettier than others, and in fact some were beautiful. Pretty or cute in grammar school, but real beauty bloomed along about the second year of high school. That was around the time when we got up enough nerve to ask them to dance. Last dance, anyway.

But it slowly dawned on us that the most attractive girls had more than just looks. There was a snap, a confidence, a smile, a personality, and something we later called "class." And sexy? Maybe that, too.

There was always that fascination with women a class or two ahead of us. (Note, the use of "women" while the girls in our class were still "girls.") Barbara Williams, I thought, was absolutely gorgeous, and when she sang her famous solo in "O Holy Night" from the balcony in the auditorium, I almost melted. The classic dazzler, as I recall, was Peggy Irvine, who just *glowed* with beauty and, like Rice Krispies, had Snap, Crackle, and Pop.

It's a real danger now, these many years later, mentioning some names and not mentioning others, but I think every guy in town adored sweet Mary Lou. Jerry Fry told me that as he watched her "mature" he began to realize that girls were different than boys.

Then, in my senior year, that bevy of beauties, the Harris girls, blew into town, as on a summer breeze, and Honey Harris, Queen of the Senior Ball, patched up my self-esteem which had suffered since kindergarten.

This all comes to mind now with the advent of Reunion Season, which is, as we know, the world's greatest motivator of weight loss. Will she or he be there, and will we know them? Pray for name tags; smile and lie a little or a lot. "You look just the same, only better." Or "Of course I recognize you." And "Too bad about old what's-his-name."

The subject has been overdone, but the fascination is still there. Let's face it: it doesn't matter how much money they have, or where they live or any of that. *It's how they look!* I mean how *we* look, or maybe how *you* look. Okay, it really gets down to how *I* look! Skin deep and all that.

Chapter 49
Reunion, Part 2

Here we are, in our late seventies, some pushing eighty, class of 1947, Pacific Grove High School.

Each reunion opens a different set of emotions, and now, with the days down to a precious few, we're wondering when to have the next. The sooner the better, and six months sounds just about right.

We read our 1947 yearbook, and laugh and cry at the same time.

We've changed, matured, in some cases grown old. The guys are a little thick in the middle, not quite as tall, and what hair we have left is now nice and white. Some look good, and some don't. To hell with clean living and exercise!

The girls now look different, but better. Pretty then, beautiful now, with the patina of love and sorrow, as well as joy and happy experience. There is a quiet charm replacing that old perkiness, and a well-tuned sense of humor and still those sweet smiles! And oh my! Just look into those lovely limpid eyes! Most of us have the faces and shapes we have earned and deserve. The ladies especially know it's not how you're built that counts, it's how you're wired.

Some of us live with physical pain, borrowed knees, hips, and elbows, and other transplanted organs, but there seems to be a quiet, happy satisfaction that we have made it this far. And truth to tell, we all seem to like each other. Old issues have mellowed and the good memories enhanced. There is still a lot of "what might have been," and in some cases "why not now," but basically we are a content bunch, remembering, remembering.

Our class had the most glorious fights, the most romantic dances, the sweetest love, the most salacious scandals, as well as the longest friendships. We quietly kid ourselves that with the sixtieth reunion now history, we look forward to the seventy-fifth. Maybe not quite, but if not, we'll meet again, around the bend.

Chapter 50
Perils Past

Those of us on the north side of seventy sometimes look back with awe, wonder, and gratitude to the Lord that we did, in fact, survive. I don't mean against those ailments and diseases that passed through our lives, but rather those dumb tricks, toys, and diversions that we now remember as stupid.

Sure, we knew that firecrackers and cherry bombs were bad, but the adrenaline rush seemed worth it. In defense of our parents and us, we really didn't know that lead and mercury were bad for us. Most of the kids my age melted lead over the kitchen stove, then poured it into molds making lead soldiers. I remember that it smelled good. At least it smelled interesting. Later, as a paperboy, those familiar fumes from the marvelous linotype brought memories of lead soldiers. Mike Ragatt salvaged lead for his soldiers from old batteries, which sounds to me like double peril. But look at Mike. Picture of health! Rides a bike, climbs mountains, and ushers at church! A submarine skipper and Santa Catalina coach, to boot! Might even have done him some good.

Then, of course, mercury, usually from old thermometers. Remember how it rolled around in your hand, then rubbed on dimes? I can't imagine anybody actually tasting it, but you know some kids did. Like "don't put beans in your ears," or worse!

Then we come to gunpowder. The best source was shotgun shells or bullets. With a good pair of pliers you could pull them apart, toss away the shot and the firing pin, and pour out the powder. I remember the "powder" as tiny little donut-shaped pieces that we used for any number of experiments. Usually just a line on the sidewalk, then lit with a match. Nice quick little blaze that left a line in the concrete. Hell to pay when Dad found out.

I never knew anybody who put out an eye with a BB gun, but the peril was there. And good grief, our chemistry sets, which did cause both noise and distress and smelled up the house…

There was also a moderate thrill in Pacific Grove to hike up the storm sewer pipes with the possible peril of a rush of water that would carry us out to sea. The rumor was that some kid from Monterey wandered up the pipe in the park across from St. Mary's and was never seen again.

I don't think kids whittle pieces of wood anymore, but we treasured our pocketknives, and I can still show you scars on both hands.

If you were able to drive the family car, or somebody else's, during World War II, you'll remember the taste of gasoline as it spurted out of the siphon hose. Even at $4 a gallon, that technique seems a lost art.

No, life isn't as dangerous as it was in the good old days.

By the way, have you seen that trick with Mentos and Diet Coke?

Chapter 51
Goodbye, Jerry

There's nothing like a funeral to focus your mind on any number of things—your own certain demise, your obituary (too late to pad it), your memorial service, those you will leave behind, and those who will leave sooner than you expect.

Most of all, as you sit there in a back pew, you realize how much you will miss your friend, and maybe how little you really appreciated him in all those years, now gone.

I knew Jerry Fry all those many summers, growing up, playing with him near his house at Caledonia Park. And then those card games in the Fry kitchen, in high school and after. We packed into the Sierra together, over Kearsarge Pass, each carrying 90 pounds, believe it or not. Mostly food, which a bear ate on the second night, and we were forced to march out early.

Jerry was class president three years at PGHS, and a career in politics seemed likely. A mayor? Certainly. But a Pacific Grove kid mayor of Monterey? Not likely!

The same old story. For several of the past few weeks I had planned to call Jerry. Just to see how he was doing, really knowing what he would say. But I wanted him to help me remember the old days: specifically, when the senior class walked away from school down to Lover's Point, Mr. Cope in hot pursuit. Hell to pay, but we recovered.

Also, what was the name of the candy store next to the theater, and the soda fountain on the same side of Lighthouse? And when did this and that happen, and what else to remember? Didn't quite get around to the call.

I had moved away after college and the Navy, and not reading the *Herald*, I missed a lot of Jerry's accomplishments. But after I came back he was willing, with all due modesty, to fill me in, but mostly about Mary and his great family.

In addition to the eternal life that he deserves, there are those honors and memories that will be around a long time. What a treasure!

While we're on the subject, get in touch with those friends you've been meaning to call. Thanks, Jerry, for the reminder.

Chapter 52
Innocence

I remember hearing that pure innocence starts downhill as soon as a baby is born. They arrive pure, clean, and without sin, or experience, for that matter, and exposure to life taints the soul. Conscience enters the picture sooner or later, and somewhere we learn right from wrong. Overlooking the "the terrible twos," I don't think modest badness starts until around kindergarten, but on into grammar school, we learn, observe, imitate, and acquire some bad habits.

Getting into the teen years, we learn and yearn and discover, gradually, lust.

It is no mean trick to get out of high school innocent and pure, fantasies notwithstanding. We were saved from indiscretions by passionate restraint, or perhaps, restrained passion, never again with a conscience so clean. Some kids smoked and some kids drank and some messed around in the backseats of cars, but Lord, not me! Not me! I was an athlete!

But then, with a glorious shout, off to college! It took some time—two or three weeks—to shake off the Puritan ethic of Pacific Grove, and truth be known, in that summer between high school and college, I at least became aware of carnal possibilities.

Now look at the current crop of potential sinners. I mean teenagers. They do things which seem to be accepted and often approved. Of course, they are all going straight to Hell, but then, maybe not! They are missing that delicious feeling of guilt, that guilt we felt in the good old days. Knowing that you had stepped over the line—just a little bit—

and gotten away with it did wonders for private self-esteem. I'm not sure if it's mentioned in the Bible, but self-righteousness is a sin in itself.

But now, these many years and many sins later, look back and cherish that sweetness of senior high school love. If we look closely, without snap judgment, we may notice a couple of high school kids— boys and girls—strolling hand in hand, swinging down the lane, lovelight in their eyes, still almost as innocent as kindergarten, not knowing that next year will be even better!

III. FICTION

Chapter 53
Costco Senior

He remembered, a long time ago, when he ran across the street in his business suit and realized he was running flat-footed, just like an old man. Now he felt lucky just to get to the other side. Lived in the back room of his daughter's house and tried to stay out of her hair. Couple of minor strokes, TIAs, and the doc said maybe another one, bigger, down the road, but not to worry. Sure.

Every day now, almost, his daughter dropped him off at Costco right after they opened at ten. He had his own card, and he'd been doing this long enough that they all knew him, always pleasant.

"Hi, Sam! How goes it today?"

He would always smile as best he could, and wave. Easier than trying to talk and get into a conversation. They considered him a harmless fixture, part of the store's personality. He never bought anything, but his daughter did.

First stop the TV area, where twenty or more different screens displayed the same sports event. He had to work hard to concentrate on just one screen or he'd get dizzy.

Around 11:00 the sample foods came out, and they all encouraged him to try a little of this and that. By noon he was pretty full and continued his hike around the store. In the old days he had run a dime store and still liked to keep up on retail and how Costco moved the merchandise.

Then a little time in the book section. They always had some sort of furniture display near the books, and he could take a break in one of their chairs. After books and furniture, up one aisle and down another.

Enjoyed the meat counter, knew they had the best in town. Produce, wines and liquors, first-class bakery, then by the freezers, around and around. He was killing time, he knew, but really did enjoy checking out the action. Had he been younger, a lot younger, he could see this would be a good place to meet people. Now it was just fun to watch. From time to time, with a practiced eye, he'd spot a little shoplifting, somebody bending over the lobster tails and slipping a package into an oversize purse. Not smart, he knew. Better to lift out of the cart back in the dog food section. One guy would pop open a bottle of booze, take two or three good hits with a straw, then restock the shelf.

Around two in the afternoon his daughter would pick him up in front of the store, but sometimes she'd walk around with him, buying what she needed. If he wasn't out in front when she arrived, she'd park and ask the crew if they had seen him.

"Saw him last by the flowers, Mrs. Kelly," and there he was. Then home for a nap.

Occasionally he liked to check out Macy's or even Home Depot, but Costco was the best.

And then one day he fell down. For some reason he couldn't get up. Mind was clear and all that, but he just couldn't push himself off the floor. Someone called 911, and he was off to the ER for observation overnight. Home the next morning. A little stiff, but could still maneuver, and all in all felt pretty good.

Costco called his daughter to see how he was, and then told her, "Mrs. Kelly, we really can't have Sam in the store anymore by himself. I know you understand."

Sam accepted the news, understood, didn't blame them, and then spent the rest of the day watching TV.

The next morning, after his daughter had left on errands, he walked to the corner and took the 42 bus to BART. He rode to San Francisco, and caught a bus out to the Golden Gate. It was a beautiful day, with no wind; he could see out to the Farallons. How many times he had cruised under that bridge... a long time ago in the Navy, and then on several fishing trips. People walked by, smiling at him, marveling at the view. Then he knew it was time to go, and he grasped the rail with both hands and tried to lift his right leg up. That didn't work, so he rested a minute, got his breath, and tried the other leg. Didn't work. He tried a little jump with both feet and couldn't even get his shoes off the deck. Nobody seemed to notice. He waited for a while and knew this wasn't going to work. He decided to go home and come back tomorrow with that little aluminum step stool in the garage. He walked back to the bus stop, tired but determined, then climbed aboard the bus and settled down.

His daughter, home from errands, wondered where he was. She checked his room and the yard, then drove to Costco. How could he have gotten there?

"But no, Mrs. Kelly, we haven't seen him."

And then the phone rang. "I'm sorry, Mrs. Kelly. It looks like he just fell asleep and passed away on the bus."

Chapter 54

I Have Robbed a Bank and I Need a Ride

Jimmy is cousin Millie's husband and is a very nice guy. Retired, a little over eighty, a few health problems, but he still gets along just fine. They live in a nice house out by the river, just about as good as it gets in Bakersfield.

A couple of years ago Millie went off for a few days to visit the grandkids in Paso Robles, and then decided to stay for a few days more. Jimmy didn't mind. He was able to fix his own dinners, and when he didn't feel like cooking he'd go down to the Woolgrowers, one of the last good Basque places, and have supper there.

Tuesday morning he was a little bored, and just a little lonesome, and he figured it was a good time to visit Wells Fargo, check his balances, deposit a couple of checks, kill a little time before lunch and his afternoon nap. Nice warm day, spring at its best.

He wheeled his big black Cadillac into the parking lot, a little off to the side in a patch of shade. As he stepped out of the car, a man approached him, walking not quickly but, it seemed to Jimmy, with purpose. The guy looked to be in his thirties, decently dressed, and maybe Latino.

"Sir," he said to Jimmy, "I have just robbed the bank and need a ride. Can you help me?"

He had one hand in his jacket pocket, maybe with a gun, and a paper bag in the other.

Jimmy, having dealt with crisis before in his life, accepted all this at face value, and said calmly, "Of course. Do you want me to drive, or would you rather?"

"I'll drive," said the guy, and away they went. In the rearview mirror Jimmy saw people pouring out of the bank pointing and shouting, and he wondered if they had his license number.

About two blocks later, down a side street and then a main artery, the guy said, politely, "My name is Abrego and I am very sorry to bother you."

"Quite all right," said Jimmy. "I wasn't doing anything anyway. And by the way, did anybody in the bank get hurt, I mean shot, or anything?"

"No," said Abrego. "Nobody was hurt. I didn't even have a gun."

He smiled a little, not seeming nervous at all, and by golly, neither was Jimmy!

Jimmy told him his name, and they shook hands.

"Jimmy," said Abrego, "would you please look in the paper bag and see if I got very much money?"

Jimmy looked and there seemed to be five or six bundles of twenties and a few loose fives and tens.

"I would guess maybe a thousand dollars. We can stop later and count it for sure. I think you are new at this game, isn't that right?"

"I've never done this before, but I need the money so bad. My wife is sick and had to quit her job. I couldn't get work, and my two kids need things and I didn't know what to do. I went a little crazy this morning, and I'll never do it again, and you are so nice to help me, and I don't know what will happen to my family if get caught!"

Jimmy was quiet for a while, and they were now driving aimlessly, it seemed, through the fields south of town. No visible pursuit, and it looked like maybe they had gotten away. Jimmy wondered why he thought "they" or "we" had gotten away, but he did feel like a partner in the heist. He thought the surveillance camera at the bank might have cooked Abrego's goose, but he didn't bring it up.

Well, crime doesn't pay, and as they headed back toward town, two police cars pulled them over, and they took Abrego away, but not until Jimmy gave him a hug and a handshake and wished him good luck.

That night when he talked to Millie he said, as usual, "Oh, not much."

He had a good meal that night at the Woolgrowers, with a glass or two of that good Basque red. The next morning he went to see Abrego in jail and found out where his family was. He promised Abrego that he would make sure they were okay. And he did.

When Abrego went before the judge, Jimmy sat behind him in the court room, and since he had had a few words with his old friend the District Attorney, he was pleased to see that he got a light sentence, first offense, family in need, and so on.

Since Jimmy's Wells Fargo account was his own damn business, Millie didn't have to know that Abrego's family was on Jimmy's payroll and that Rosa got well and got her job back. And when Abrego got out, Jimmy helped him get a job at one of the hotels downtown.

Millie still visits the grandkids in Paso Robles, and Jimmy still has supper at the Woolgrowers. He still checks his balances at Wells Fargo. He does, however, park his car on the other side of the bank, a little closer to the door.

Chapter 55
A Friday Afternoon

Nine Ponds was a semi-secluded wooded place up the hill from the high school. Old springs seeped into nine small ponds, although I don't remember anybody actually counting them.

There was a path through the bramble up to Forest Avenue, and this is where the high school junior boys went to smoke. The seniors, with territorial rights, smoked across the street from the high school in a lot vacant except for a few pines and bushes. It was known as the Tobacco Plantation.

One Friday afternoon after class, three junior boys were puffing their Camels in Nine Ponds, trying to blow smoke rings, coughing and spitting, bragging about anything they could think of, and fantasizing about the senior girls. They were just about to light their second cigarettes when down the path from Forest came Neona Nichols on her way home. She lived on the street above, but this was a handy shortcut, through Nine Ponds.

Neona was a sophomore, and today she would have been described as "challenged." Back then, she was called "odd," and indeed she was. Although she had no particular friends, the other girls were nice to her, and the teachers were kind and understanding in her direction. She was very thin, pale, and plain. Her hair was tied back in a bow, and she dressed very simply. Neona sometimes giggled without apparent reason; very shy, she blushed and looked away in the presence of the boys. Wherever she went she carried her books in front of her, hiding her chest. It did not appear that there was anything there yet to hide. She did smile often, but very seldom spoke.

On this Friday afternoon she looked down the path, saw the boys, hesitated, and started to turn around and head back to Forest.

"Neona, Neona!" John called out. "Come on back! We want to talk to you!"

Clyde said, "Oh let her go."

"No, this could be fun!"

Neona stopped and turned around and slowly walked toward them, staying on the path, holding her books, looking down.

"Come on, Neona. We won't hurt you! Here, try a cigarette."

She shook her head no.

"Come on. We won't tell and I'll bet you'll like it."

"Come on, John. Let her go!"

She shifted her books to her left arm, slowly reached and took the Camel, then dropped it and started to walk down the path.

"Hey, wait! We've got a secret! Tony Angelo says he likes you!"

Neona turned again, smiled, and started to giggle. Her face was sweaty, a tear or two down her dusty cheeks.

"Just one more thing, Neona, and we'll let you go. We'll even tell Tony you're nice. Now we won't tell anybody, but right now, pull down your panties and let's see what you got!"

Tom and Clyde both said, "Jesus, John. Let her go!"

"Come on, Neona. Just for a second. We won't touch you!"

She quickly put her books down on a log, with her left hand she pulled up her dress, and with her right pulled her pants down to her knees, exposing a pathetic, pale, skinny body.

The boys were silent. She pulled up her panties, smoothed her dress, picked up her books, and fluttered on up the path.

Nobody said a word, and the boys walked back up to Forest Avenue and headed down the hill to town. The incident was never mentioned.

The Nine Ponds have all dried up, and homes built there. Junior boys now smoke someplace else.

Chapter 56
Trapped

As usual, the line to the ladies' toilets—in this case *Damas*—was at least twice as long as the *Hombres*, and Miss Quilken was relieved to say the least when it was her turn in the stall.

The tour bus had bounced through the spectacular Mallorcan hills for what seemed like hours, and Miss Quilken hardly heard the chatter of the guide, so acute was her distress. When they finally lurched to stop at the "fabulous and very ancient" farm complex, the guide gave them ten minutes before they were to stroll the gardens and the rest.

The stall was clean and private, and now, feeling much better, Miss Quilken stood, adjusted her clothes, and pushed purposely on the door. The latch seemed to stick.

Ah, maybe it needed to be slid more to the left while pushing just a little on the door.

Miss Quilken tried to rattle the door, now aware of the distress of the other ladies waiting—there were only two stalls—and in a brave voice said loudly, "I'm sorry to take so long but the latch seems stuck. Could you perhaps push on the door a little?"

Lucille from Texas said, "Wait a minute, honey, try moving the latch the other way."

It was not a very warm day, but Miss Quilken began to sweat, and then, not used to closed spaces, said very loudly, "Please help me get *out* of here!"

Ladies moving slowly in and out of the next stall or moving from one foot to the other had lots of advice and encouragement, but mostly to Just Calm Down!

Lucille from Texas understood that Miss Quilken—"Isn't she the one in the blue jacket?" "Yes, I think so"—had really freaked out, as she put it, and that beyond reason, kicking and screaming wasn't doing any good. Lucille from Texas went to find help. Miss Quilken, sobbing, gave up and sank to the floor next to the toilet.

In the next stall, the toilet flushed and the door opened and shut without incident.

Daniel from Omaha, a retired fireman, having finished in *Hombres*, heard the commotion in *Damas* walked in to see if he could help. He jiggled the door without success and tried to reassure the sobbing Miss Quilken to try and stay calm.

The top of the stall and the door went all the way to the ceiling, but Daniel noted about a fourteen-inch opening between the bottom of the door and the tile floor. Although the idea did not appeal to him, he knew his duty, took off his jacket, and head first, on his back, with arms outstretched, attempted to slide into the stall.

Miss Quilken, now well beyond reason, was not reassured by the sight of Daniel's hands, arms, and head, his face now somewhat contorted. Convinced she was about to die, she sobbed even louder, and then blessedly, fainted, the toilet in the next stall continuing to flush.

It had been a long time since Daniel had crawled under a stall door, and it seemed that he not only underestimated the size of the opening, he had also underestimated his girth—belly, that is—and he got stuck. He was also so tightly jammed he couldn't move in either direction, and in fact so tight he couldn't speak to ask for help but was only able to moan, albeit, very expressively.

His wife Marge, sensing the predicament, hollered for help and tried to pull him out, but his shoe came off and she fell backward, not hurt, but mad as hell. She would rather have seen the rest of the ancient farm, but she cared about Daniel—didn't give a damn about

148

Miss Quilken—and as Daniel had grown quiet, she hoped he hadn't died. He had not.

The tour guide then stormed into *Damas* wanted to what in hell was going on. Her English was adequate to express her displeasure and then, to save the day, a gardener arrived with a hammer, smashed the latch, pulled out Daniel, and opened the door.

Chapter 57
By Jesus

The Reverend Alan Sumner faced a big Dilemma with a capital D. Like most good ministers, even those with successful churches, he was under constant, niggling pressure from one pew or another. Yesterday one of his strongest and most loyal members pointed out that, even though his sermons were better than ever, attendance was dwindling and there were some murmurs heard at the coffee hour on Sunday.

"Just a thought, Reverend. Got to keep the place full!"

He told his wife Lorna what the story was, and she said, "By Jesus! You know the reason, and by Jesus, you've got to fix it!" It should be noted that Lorna often said "By Jesus," but it was said as a prayer, really, not as a blasphemy.

The problem was the Tuck twins, identical sisters in their mid-sixties, both happily divorced and living together on the family farm just outside of town. They were proud of the fact that their father was descended from a slave family, had homesteaded and put it all together. He'd handpicked cotton himself and all that. They had been good, loyal parishioners, sitting quietly halfway back on the right side. They sang loudly, with fervor, and knew all the words.

The problem started about the middle of last year when they began to talk to each other throughout the entire service. It started in a quiet, conversational tone, perhaps as their hearing began to fail, or whatever, but by now they talked at a level that reached every corner of the sanctuary, including the pulpit and the choir loft. The contents and subjects were the sort of thing you might discuss after church, maybe on the way home, but no, they appeared to be unaware of any impropriety and happily rattled on about Amy's hat, or Selma Jones's wig, and the noisy three-year-old in the back. While Alan's sermons were usually powerful and well-delivered, the twins often lost interest and a few minutes after "May the words of my mouth" they started in on the state of the nation, the unusual weather, and whatever happened to that young girl who ran off with the teacher. There were always shushes, sometimes even louder than the Tucks' conversation, but they didn't seem to notice and prattled happily along.

Now the Reverend Sumner was an experienced preacher, and things like kids crying, coughing spells, or candy wrappers didn't bother him. Nor did little things like Mavis Morgan, well into her eighties, standing every Sunday when he asked for birthdays. "Happy Birthday, Mavis," he would smile, and so did everybody else. He even survived the day when Agnes Porter, a little low on her medications, strolled up to the pulpit, made sure the speaker was on, said "Bullshit" loud and clear, and then quietly returned to her seat.

And old Simpson Whittle, a real pseudo-sinner who didn't know a whorehouse from a hardware store, loved to get up, testify and confess, come forward and be saved over and over again. Alan preferred real sinners, those who had honestly raised hell, but sooner or later came to know the Lord. Like that Monday afternoon when he found the sexton and the organist in "fond embrace" in the choir loft. They quietly promised to repent, and that was fine with him. (They later married.) Lorna said she always wondered where the word sexton came from.

This was all part of the fabric of worship, fellowship, and brotherly, sisterly understanding. But when loud conversation...well, you get the picture. Prayerful meditation became almost impossible, and some people stomped out before the benediction, glaring at the "magpies." Worse yet, some of the most loyal began to stay away, preferring to worship at United Presbyterian across town.

Now this would seem like an easy situation to correct. A kind word to the twins, a special blessing, or as Lorna Sumner told her husband, "By Jesus, tell them to shut up!"

But Alan couldn't take the chance, for any number of reasons.

Just last year, about the time the problem started, Avon Oil and Gas drilled five very successful gas wells on the twins' acreage, each well named by the twins for a book in the Bible. Genesis One, Exodus Two, etc. And the royalties rolled in, big-time.

Nobody had the nerve to suggest that the twins share this with the Lord, or even the church, but suggestion or not, from that time on the twins dropped $500 checks in the plate every single Sunday. Five hundred each, no more, no less.

You can do the math, and so did the Reverend Alan Sumner. He also knew that most of those who stomped out, never to return, had dropped a lot less than that in their lifetimes!

The situation got worse, with louder remarks, comments on the sermon, and even laughs at any minor misstatements by the Reverend Sumner. Needless to say, he was making more misstatements than he ever had before.

Finally, as attendance fell to less than half, Lorna Sumner did some math herself, and despite the $500 contributions (each), she began to have some concern—not only for the church, God forbid, but by Jesus, their own retirement!

One Sunday afternoon, after a particularly noisy service, she not only threatened to go to United Pres herself, but by Jesus, if Alan didn't do something, *she* surely would!

This did focus things for Alan, and he phoned the Tucks and asked if he could call on them that evening.

"Ladies," he said. "First of all I want to thank you personally for your generous support of the church. Central Baptist would not be the same without you. You are in my prayers (no kidding) every day and I know the Lord appreciates your commitment."

While the Tuck sisters did prattle and chatter, they were not stupid, and they sensed something was on the table. And indeed it was. With a prayer to God in his heart, Alan went on to explain how much he personally appreciated their comments and spiritual outpouring during Sunday service. There were, however, some in the congregation who did not understand or appreciate their rich Southern heritage and verbal contribution to worship. Alan began to sweat and prayed that he had opened this can of worms on the right note.

"As a matter of fact," he blurted on, "you may have noticed that quite a few people are no longer in church, and rumor has it that they have moved over to United Pres!"

At this point he had completely lost his nerve, mumbled again his thanks for their support, and stumbled out the door.

The next morning he was still a wreck, convinced he had blown the whole deal.

"By Jesus, I hope not!" said Lorna.

Then the phone rang and the Tuck sisters asked if he could visit them again that afternoon. Fearing the worst, he knocked on the farmhouse door and sat down to a tall glass of iced tea. Just what he needed.

The Tucks had a way of starting and finishing each other's sentences, but the thoughts came out in order, clearly and smoothly. First, they deeply appreciated his letting them know and were so sorry that they had hardly been able to sleep. But they talked about it this morning and decided they would try United Pres themselves—his heart sank—but just for a few Sundays, or at least until they had driven the drifters back to Alan's and their church!

Then, they promised, when they came back to their place in the pew, they would keep their mouths shut—except for the hymns! And just one more thing, they would drop their $500 checks (each) at the church office on Saturdays. All most confidential.

The Reverend Sumner didn't quite know how to handle this, still shaken to the core, but suggested the three of them bow in a prayer of Thanksgiving.

He knew it was time to leave, but as he stood, the Tucks said, "Just one *more* thing."

They had called their attorney that morning and directed that all the income from Deuteronomy Five go directly to Central Baptist from that time on, and oh, five percent of that to the pastor's retirement fund.

He raced home, hugged Lorna, and told her the news.

"By Jesus," she said quietly.

Chapter 58
Verse

My grandson is handsome, tall, and autistic.
They say, high-functioning.
He starts his private morning with a song, a prayer,
And a daily plan.

His world is private, but he sometimes lets me in.

# # # #

The old chair stands in the corner now, seldom sat on except by the cat.
But in its two hundred or more years how many bottoms, dozens? hundreds?
Rested there. It looks and feels like old pine, somewhat ragged from forgotten finishes
And seasons left outside. I remember an earthy yellow, then covered by my dad in a
Bright red. Little odd traces still there. Great-great-grandfather Dinsmore was a
New England chairmaker and his name is carved under the seat. This is one of my
Treasures, and who will take care of it when I'm gone?

# # # #

Love is an accident planned by God.
The rest is up to us.

1338184

Made in the USA